Primordial
Grace

D1720239

Also by Robert and Rachel Olds

Luminous Heart of the Earth:
A Survival Guide for Original Heart

Luminous Heart of Inner Radiance:
Drawings of the Tögal Visions

Water Drawn Before Sunrise:
A Journey of Return

PRIMORDIAL GRACE

Earth

Original Heart

and the

Visionary Path of

Radiance

ROBERT & RACHEL OLDS

HEART SEED PRESS

All practices referred to in this book were used by the authors except where noted. Readers use at their own risk any of the information and advice the book offers, and they should carefully study and clearly understand the material before any such use. Anyone using this book is personally responsible for his or her own spiritual life. No one should practice the visionary path of radiance without first being able to clearly experience original heart. The authors and publishers assume no responsibility for any injury or loss suffered in connection with use of this book.

Heart Seed Press
www.acircleisdrawn.org
email: robert.rachel@acircleisdrawn.org

ISBN 978-0-9831945-5-2

Illustrations copyright © Robert & Rachel Olds
Book design by Robert & Rachel Olds

*Dedicated to all Earth peoples and to all those who are choosing
to return to a life blended with our First Mother.*

primordial grace,

beyond all language or culture,

pure potential, an intent whose reflection

manifests as the natural world,

arising in concentric spheres of influence,

curving lines through undefined space,

a dewdrop falling into the surface of a pond.

We gratefully acknowledge all our guides, everyone and everything, the vast display of this wondrous vision we find ourselves within and the path of primordial grace, the union of the vision we call this life, original heart, and the transcendent visions of radiance. Friends, plants, animals, relatives, Earth, sky, fire, water, air, and space all carry precious teachings ready to be unveiled and revealed if you are open and allowing. We thank you all from our deepest hearts.

Contents

Opening Your Heart   73

The Spiritual Path   111

Original Heart Original Nature   139

PART II

The Visionary Path of Radiance

Primordial Joy   187

Threshold

Primordial grace, the great perfection woven throughout the fabric of being, offers always a way home, in and through the natural radiance of the origin itself. The practices of opening to this sacred wholeness arose out of direct experience in the wilderness long before humans turned from the Earth and created structures of separation. We want to encourage reconnection with the original roots of this primordial path and bring these practices back to the Earth, their natural home. Particularly now in these times of great upheaval brought on by human insistence on remaining apart from the natural world, we need to make a different choice by embracing the teachings that are all around us manifesting naturally as the vision that is this life, letting go of separation, reconnecting with the Earth, and acknowledging the radiant intent at the heart of all being as our way home.

The return to origin is part of a natural wholeness basic to human experience, a wholeness accepted and understood as the way things are by original hunter-gatherer peoples. The resolution of the path of primordial grace is at root a profoundly indigenous experience, natural to the human heart and to the Earth, woven throughout the fabric of being. This is the true perspective of the path, primordial, beyond language and culture, beyond all concept and doctrine, seamless with the intent of essence.

We saw during our nine year retreat that other practitioners around us who were approaching the path from the more limited perspective of mind and concepts born of separation from the Earth were having difficulty with their practice, and we began to consider how we could express our experience in a way that could help them. From the perspective of the final resolution of the path, we looked at our lives and the choices we made along the way. Your spiritual path is not separate from your life. We sifted through the events that were pivotal for us and had enabled us along the path when so many other practitioners were having difficulties. In our memoir, *Water Drawn Before Sunrise,* we wrote about the events and choices that reflected not only our spiritual experience but how we grappled with the weighted concepts of belief and power and separation that have come to overshadow the natural radiance of being. And in writing from our direct experience, we developed a way of speaking about the path outside the constraints of doctrine and culture that have afflicted spiritual growth since our collective fall away from the Earth.

This book is a guide to the primordial path already laid out in your heart leading you back to origin. Part I is a revised and expanded version of our previous book *Luminous Heart of the Earth: A Survival Guide for Original Heart*, reunited here with Part II our practice manual for the visionary path of radiance. We are presenting the practice of radiance from its original perspective of sacred Earth, a perspective that is sorely needed now at this crucial time in the life of our mother planet. This is a guide to the natural wholeness of the complete path, including essential preparations, instructions, and practical advice for acknowledging original heart and the practice of the visions of radiance, written from our direct experience of the completion of the path of radiance.

If you know the general lay of the land up ahead on the trail you can come to it better prepared than if you are hampered by misconception and rumor. From the standpoint of personal practice, in becoming aware of the full scope of the trail you are more likely to respect qualities of Earth and heart in yourself and all around you, which will not only help your practice but help heal the life of our times as well.

We offer this book as a seed text of hope, to reawaken the natural path to oneness through original heart, the Earth, and the visions of radiance, in a time of unparalleled darkness of humanity's willful push toward extinction. There is a seed ready to sprout in the rubble of this age, and within the condition of being a seed is the energy to live and grow, to reestablish the natural connection with primordial grace.

If our words resonate with your heart, put them into practice; learn to live with our First Mother, not just in a physical way, but feeling her through your whole being. This is a survival manual and a prayer for the coming age, a prayer for the luminous aware original heart of all life.

As our present age is coming to an end, and our mother planet is approaching crises of unthinkable proportions, there is an urgent need for humans to once again understand and feel from our hearts and blend with the natural order of being. We need to see clearly where we as a species stand now, acknowledge our destructive and disastrous choices and the distance we need to cross to free ourselves from the structures we have built to circumvent the indwelling wholeness of the natural universe. We have a responsibility to dismantle the elaborate architecture of our self-imposed exile from the Earth and rejoin the natural flow of life. The future of the entire sacred circle of life may well depend on our willingness to return. No part is ever truly separate from the whole. We have never been alone. The universe is grace, ready to welcome us home

Return from the Fall

Our Earth is facing a period of mass extinction because of a fundamental lie, the terrible lie we polish every day. The more we destroy the Earth, the more we polish and shine and exaggerate the lie, the less we question it. We have held this lie ever since we first decided to forget our Mother Earth, taking an aberrant path of the mind turning away from the heart connection with all life.

Having received everything, needing nothing, our ancestors walked away from what is generously offered by the Earth within a blended existence, and set themselves apart, considering themselves special, unique, and above all creation. Within the fluid allowing nature of Earth, taking advantage of that inherent freedom, humans reasoned for power and made a dark and evil decision. In separating from the natural flow of all things, they set in motion a power completely alien to all life and the lie was born. The mind forced a cloak over the heart and truth. Reason created its own reality overriding the open and allowing nature of Earth. And by willingly cutting their senses away from the direct knowing of original heart, our ancestors ensnared themselves in the lie of the mind and a warped cycle of deception.

The motivation for this would be hard to understand if it were only in the long forgotten past.

But this decision to follow the lie is with us every moment of our lives. Original heart, the heart breath of the fabric of being, is all around us and within us, and at every moment we face the same choice of being with our Mother Earth or turning from her to live the lie. Even now when our Earth is in peril due to our lie, we hold to the lie and believe in our greatness, thinking that technology will solve the problems we have created. Our arrogance grows with the lie. We revel in our splendor hiding behind our magnificence so we do not see the lie, our evolutionary journey to socio/psychopathic insanity, dominating and destroying all life.

The lie is regenerated when we acquiesce to our present condition; when we believe that there is no other way but to continue the lie. We are separated from most of the death caused by the lie. We wash our hands and find solace in our ability to stop using plastic bags, or by recycling or insulating our homes, but since the fall, the blood on our hands is made fresh moment by moment within the lie.

But even at this late hour, within every moment there exists a chance to return to a blended way of being. This return is not just a physical return to a natural life. It is returning to our hearts and turning away from the lie, to live again reunited within the openness of original heart within all that naturally arises.

Returning from the fall brings us back into relation with the intent of essence expressed as the radiance of this world. With all life on our Mother Earth now facing extinction, there could be no greater prayer for her than this return to original heart, a fluid openness blended with the nurturing flow of all manifestation, a heartfelt knowing that can allow and be with the unfolding of the world. One true moment of this is worth countless lifetimes embittered by the lie. The reunion with original heart and the fabric of being is freshness, kindness, blessing, and grace, so simple and omnipresent, but first we must let go of the lie and acknowledge our right to return to authentic being, our right to spiritual growth and spiritual maturity.

Divine Treason

The ripening of the spiritual path has become ensnared in concepts and doctrine. Enlightenment, realization, liberation, fruition are now concepts within the mind. There are no names for or ownership of the natural blended experience of oneness. There are no laws or rules beyond the embrace of what naturally arises, an openness expanding outward to oneness, a love that cannot be confined or ruled by human manipulation, a divine love that dances out this glorious universe, this glorious Earth.

Spiritual growth is a living process, not an esoteric act performed by religious elites, nor is it attainable only through their authority. You need no intermediary to meet the ground of being directly in your own experience. Returning to origin is a spiritual maturing as natural as a plant growing, blossoming, fruiting, and setting seed, and just as plant and seed are inherent in each other, spiritual completion is woven throughout the fabric of being.

We are all here in this life to mature. Each heart holds an ember, a living seed of the fruition of this dynamic process of becoming, a fruition natural to us and to all life, an embrace of all being, generous and open. The scope of this birthright is far beyond the words and mythologies built around enlightenment by religious structures that have helped devalue heart-based human interaction, through reinforcing patterns for consolidation of power and wealth for the benefit of the dominating class.

Cultures based on hierarchies and exploitation, the lies born of separation, must limit the range of authentic experience of those exploited in order to control them. Our birthright was once a natural aspect of life; an experience lived through the heart, and is all but forgotten now. The suffering that people experience comes directly out of our loss due to dominator cultures, the enforced forgetting of our connection with the fabric of being. Suffering is an integral aspect of dominator cultures: it is the suffering born of humans who have become separate from the woven beatitude of life.

Divine treason is to accept our spiritual worthiness. We have the same intrinsic right to direct experience of spiritual growth as we have to economic, social, and environmental justice. These issues are not separate. The inequalities are maintained by the same mythologies. The rulers, whether heads of state, bankers, priests, lamas, CEOs, or the laws of reason, science and technology, are not divine. They have merely usurped this power and claimed it for their own. Treason is divine, to accept that the human heart has a natural capacity to blend with the Source, the All by any name, and that we can all return home to a heart blended with the fabric of being and support each other in that returning. The flawed being that dominator societies call human nature is not our true face. It is the true face of the dominator's mentality with all the cruelty that entails. We look in their mirrors and see what they want us to see. Look deeper into your true heart and see what we really are and can be, one with the fabric of being, naturally generous and caring in kinship with all life.

To experience this divine embrace we each need to return to a life directed by and through the deepest part of our heart. We need to let go of internal domination by our own minds as well as by external dominators. When we give our minds rulership over our hearts we leave ourselves open to enslavement by other forces. Freeing ourselves of this takes a great deal of personal responsibility, courage, and steadfastness to persevere in the face of the overwhelmingly deformed and heartless cultures that surround us, but it can be done even now at this last hour, individually and together.

A madness afflicts humanity, a disease that has been growing for close to ten thousand years. This madness, this disease is the mind of reason dominating over the heart. We no longer trust the wordless intuitive knowing of our deepest heart, so vastly different from linear reason, and have to think to know. We have to think how we feel, and we have to think how we decide. We think our emotions, our compassion, our loving kindness. We think our spiritual experience and our meditation. We even think we are coming from our hearts. Dominated by our minds, we think our whole life experience and willingly create a world based on dominators and those who are dominated.

Dominator societies require that 99% of the people within a given culture allow themselves to be dominated. We may feel that we are being coerced, or we may be in denial about the extent of our exploitation and the mechanisms that support it, but the exploitive systems do not work without our compliance. This has been accomplished by cultural conditioning that elevates mind over heart and uses concepts, laws, and precepts to override the natural empathy that sees, hears, and feels clearly the suffering imposed on the many in the name of the few, whether for political, religious, or economic power. Without the innate wisdom and perceptions of the heart to guide the mind, we are literally out of touch. We lose our connection to our truth sense and become very susceptible to exploitation through fear and fabrication.

Fear is the principle mechanism through which dominator cultures function. Fear is often induced by physical force and cruelty at first, but the most effective fear lives within the mind of each of us, through concepts and illusions that uphold the preeminence of mind, isolating us and feeding the fears and hierarchies, the lies of separation, from within.

When we live in fear, we cling to the lure of safety and protection that the dominators promise us, even at the price of our freedom. We become afraid of anything outside the terms of the established order, anything unusual, unexpected, different, or disorderly. We cut ourselves off from our own authenticity, our own possibly unpredictable inner power, which at any moment could put us outside the boundaries of the alleged safety zones. When we live in fear, all that we can do is point the finger of blame and judgment, reinforcing the criterion that divides us from our hearts and from each other and maintains the prison walls of our illusory protection.

Original heart, naturally free, naturally one with the fabric of being, is not afraid. Within every human heart, however veiled, is a call for a true revolution of heart, a radical call to reinstate original heart in human experience and re-inhabit genuine compassion and caring born of direct experience, the kinship with all life so familiar to original peoples. This intuitive empathy, the natural fluid expression of the heart blending with another, is very different from the mentally constructed forms of behavior promoted by dominator social and religious structures caught up in maintaining the lie, the very structures that are designed to turn people, animals, plants, and the Earth into objects to be exploited for the benefit of the ruling class whose guidelines are designed to keep the exploited complicit with their limited lot.

The call within the heart is for an egalitarian, circular re-visioning of the future that includes a remembering of the way humans could be and were for hundreds of thousands of years before the advent of our disastrous top down exploitive cultures. This is a call to remember who we are and can be as a species, to reclaim our place within the entire sacred vision we call life. We know how to do this. We have been conditioned for generations to accept separation as the so-called human condition, but inside every one of us is a natural connection with the oneness of being, ready to express itself in countless acts of genuine relating.

We can re-member ourselves into the circle of life. Now is the time to return to the way of original heart blended with the Earth, and with the Earth as our guide, return to the Source, the fabric of being that dances out our Earth in all its myriad forms of beauty. This is a call to free all aspects of life from enslavement by the mind and its lineages of domination. With courage born of a blended heart, become one with the ground of being through direct experience, through the heart with the heart of all, life as a spiritual path blended with this Earth, blended within this divine dance.

Returning to origin, the natural blended experience of oneness, is coming home into the primordial radiance of this world, coming home to the natural radiance in each heart, free of the corrupting structures of domination that divide us from ourselves, from each other, and from the Earth. The Earth is the basic ground on which our lives and our spiritual practice evolve. Come home to the Earth, blended with the fabric of being, walking a courageous path with our First Mother as our guide.

PART I

Earth
and
Original Heart

Intent of Essence

The early spring air was soft and bright. The shadows held the lingering cold of winter, but the midmorning sunlight laid a kindly warmth on our shoulders as we stood on the grassy bank of the old logging road cut into the side of the mountain. The huge old madrone rooted on the slope nearby was still laden with an overabundance of bright red berries, but its usually glossy green leaves were withering; the old sentinel was dying. We looked out over the steep narrow valley that had been our cloister for eight years. The flank of the mountain dropped off sharply below us, and through a gap between tall grey trunks of Douglas fir, we could see the river sparkling in the morning light and cars moving along the highway that followed the river's winding on the other shore. We heard the familiar rumble of heavy machinery from the rock quarry as a dump truck came into view far below;

like a slow-bodied beetle or a toy truck it crawled across the uneven floor of the gravel pit. The rugged mountains that held this valley in a tight embrace were still covered with snow, but the willows along the river were beginning to quicken with a breath of green in their swelling buds.

The night before, we had completed the primordial path of radiance. After years of intense practice and many more years of letting go, we had reached the true return, the point of origin, the beginning and the end. Now we stood on the old logging road in the warm sun in early spring, enfolded in the earliest moments of our return. We were embraced within a great joy, a joy all encompassing, inseparable from the oneness at the heart of the path. The morning light, the river, the valley, the trees, the new stems of green grass and shoots of wild flowers pushing up through dried leaves of last year's growth, the poignancy of the sudden explosive sounds from the rock crusher in the quarry pit and the jake-braking logging trucks on the highway below reverberating in the soft spring air so full of awakening life, the tender beauty of the radiance intertwined with the anguished cries of the world of separation blind to the effulgent grace of the heart of origin surrounding it at every moment.

Essence

Primordial essence is beyond all aspects of this world, beyond all beliefs, all concepts, all perspectives, and all experience, a luminous knowingless knowing that cannot be defined, a primordial purity of intent that is beyond emptiness and spacious beyond all concepts of space, absolute potential, neither tangible nor intangible, yet its expression is everywhere.

This intent of absolute potential beyond all knowing bursts forth like the corona of a star from a blue-black centerless depth, kindling itself into radiance, a continuous spontaneous birthing of the arising weave of the fabric of being. Both the potential and the radiance of essence are present in everything and everyone, even the tiniest insect.

Radiance

The radiance blossoming forth from the essence, the spontaneous unceasing dynamic expression, blooming in myriad ways is the great compassion. This radiance, this compassion, is not random; it is a direct manifestation of the intent of the essence, an intent for all beings to reflect back to origin. The specific, compassionate intent that creates the entire world vision we find ourselves within begins with light, a spontaneous continuity of the essence and its radiance. The light then shapes itself into myriad rainbow colors and countless circles or spheres of being that are free and undefined, yet they form the continuum of all manifest experience as color, shape, and light. The mind defines and labels, changing and reordering its perception of what is naturally manifest into the holding patterns of time and space. Then this realm of light appears as the spatially defined and bordered solidities of the familiar world. When the radiance is perceived directly in the primordial path of light without these hindering factors, you come to a direct experience of oneness beyond any notion of oneness, living light free of the borders of intellect, seen purely from the light of the heart.

The radiance we call this world is sacred. Everything is already naturally consecrated as an expression of the essence. The Earth, trees, plants, rivers, clouds, and sky, colors, odors, tastes, textures, and sounds, all manifestations of the essence, large and small, partake of the source from which they arise. The expression of this world as the intent of the essence does not arise as an illusion to deceive. It does not arise as delusion to make us suffer, or to drive us to turn away or escape. Nor is it just a dream to be seduced by or to be tossed aside. This expression of the essence is a vision, a sacred vision with a living intent woven into the fabric of our being. The brilliance and the core essence are never separate. This unity is beyond time or space, beyond concepts, yet it can be seen, experienced, felt, responded to, and acknowledged, to complete the reflection of its return.

The arising brilliance of this world as an expression of a pure intent can be seen and felt most clearly in the natural world outside human manipulation. The signs of this radiance are everywhere: in the night sky, in a rainbow, in the sun and moon, in the elemental interplay of water, fire, Earth, wind, and space. This natural brilliance is also found within your heart, and just as the marvel of a seed settled in a nurturing bed of soil sprouts, grows, and transforms, the luminous seed of light already settled in your heart can sprout and grow, initiating the particular cycle of return that is the visionary path of radiance.

The natural world is a fluid movement. Interrelated cycles of change appear as the arising and fading rhythms of experience, and similar to bubbles on the surface of a pond, these manifest phenomena have no power to remain, due to the ceaseless transitory nature of their arising. And so the splendor of this life includes decline and decay. They are natural and necessary aspects of the cycles of change just as composting builds rich soil.

Everything that manifests in our experience, the joys and the difficulties, the choices and the ability to choose, are all expressions of the compassion of the essence. Great compassion is a fertile dynamic environment for growth. Hot and cold, up and down, near and far, fast and slow, night and day, birth and death, Earth and sky, are all aspects of the manifest dance of the essence moving us to return to origin. The complementary forces all around us provide support within which we learn and grow. The problem is not the dualistic quality of our experience; the problem is holding and clinging to any part of this dynamic whole, hindering the natural fluidity of the interactions and restricting the potential for growth.

Holding and clinging arise from an illusory sense of separation, the ignorance that manifests as self-identity. All beings have a personal sphere of being, an avenue through which they experience and choose, and are part of the great primordial compassion at the same time. Not acknowledging this inherent unity leads to clinging and the feeling of separation. The cycle is never ending, unless you embrace a spiritual path of letting go that cleans and polishes the inner surface of your sphere until it becomes open like the sky. Then, like the rainbow surface of a bubble growing thinner and thinner, it pops, and there is no more sphere, only a seamless all.

This whole world is a sacred vision, the radiance of the essence arising naturally, spontaneously, here, abundantly, and within this abundance every being has the potential to let go of separation and return to the unity of oneness. It is here for you to touch, it is calling you. The only reason we are here is to heed this call to return to origin. And so, an important initial step on any spiritual path is taking responsibility for your thoughts and actions, for how you respond to the miraculous vision we call this world, taking responsibility to undo the patterns of separation that hold you and regain the connection that has been covered over but never really lost, to recognize and nurture the seed of radiance in your heart.

Openness of Earth

Ask yourself, what is your purpose in this life? What would you be willing to do to truly follow the path of primordial grace to the ultimate goal of realizing what is already abiding in your heart, coming to the point of complete union, no separation, the dissolution of all concepts, habitual patterns, and emotions? How strong is your intent to traverse the full length of the path for all life, for every aspect of this amazing vision, not only for yourself?

The intent to benefit outside of self is crucial for the spiritual path. As natural as the caring of a mother for her child, this intent is already within you whether you are a man or a woman. You do not have to take a vow, just accept right now, right where you are, that this nurturing quality is indwelling in your heart, and allow it to radiate outward for all life. This inherent kindness is the same as the functional underlying kindness of the intent of the essence manifesting as the Earth, and this kindness includes the ripening of whatever seed is sown. Selfish actions and motivations bring conditions of increasing separation and arrested spiritual growth. Many people in Western culture are afraid of the Earth, afraid of directly experiencing the elemental aspects of life, and afraid of confronting the results of their choices and actions as reflected back to them by the Earth. We as a culture have preferred the illusion of autonomy and cut ourselves off from the depth of the nurturing quality abiding within, with disastrous results for our First Mother and ourselves. In an increasingly digitalized urbanized world, the choice to return to the Earth as the ground of spiritual practice is a crucial one, and participating with the generous heart of the essence as the path becomes a tangible prayer for the future of all life. We already know how to care, how to reach out, how to connect outside of self. These qualities are indwelling in us now, we need only to remember ourselves back into the circle of life.

To do this we need to realize in our hearts that we are one with the Earth, and we need to be able to surrender to the faithful, kindly energies already in our hearts. We need to acknowledge and accept that there is a kindness of intent here, both in the Earth and in ourselves, and this intent expresses itself through the same qualities traditionally attributed to the Earth that are the very attributes of heart that we need to recognize and cultivate for the seed of oneness to grow, bloom, and set the seed of fruition.

The Earth responds dynamically, naturally abundant and effulgent. Although we tend to experience the Earth as solid and firm ground, the actual growing layer of the soil is in a continually responsive, fertile state of transformation. The Earth is unconditional openness, allowing any choice to bear fruit. The Earth is unwavering devotion, nurturing all appearances as expressions of the essence. The Earth is absolute humility, receptive to all. These attributes of Earth, responsive, accepting, devoted, and humble are interactive and mutually supportive. They are all qualities of the same fundamental receptive openness that is a natural aspect of the essence and is all-pervasive within the manifest world. This is original heart, present here for us to recognize and learn from. It is particularly evident in the Earth, and it is already in every heart. Just as the intent to benefit outside of self is a reflection of the larger intent of the essence, the receptive openness that we can feel within the Earth and in our hearts is a direct connection with the essence, and once it is acknowledged it can be cultivated through the choices we make in our lives. We are not alone. We will be welcomed by all life if we choose to come home to sacred Earth.

Responding

Being receptive is not being passive: it is an active willingness to relate with the radiance of the essence that is manifesting ceaselessly, outwardly and inwardly. It is a direct response from your heart, a direct involvement with the very fabric of our world, a blended acknowledgement. Responding is a relational empathic experience, participating with the call and response that is ongoing and fluid all around you, not a construct of the mind but a surrender of the mind's control over the heart, a surrender that allows an open dance within your heart and the heart of all. The willingness to respond is the basis for taking responsibility for the choices you make and learning from them, taking responsibility for being part of the Earth, taking responsibility for your own life and relating with the myriad lives around you with a nurturing heart.

Allowing

This responding leads naturally to a fluid, allowing mind, soft and gentle, that does not hold or grasp onto situations, concepts, habits, and emotions and does not deny or cling. This mind is willing to listen to and follow the heart. It is willing to allow the heart to be open like the Earth, accepting anything and everything without judgment. The Earth is an absolute mother willing to allow her children to discover and experience so that they can learn directly and viscerally from the results of their actions even though they may cause her great pain. The Earth teaches you if you are willing to allow the teachings in, willing to allow an openness for learning to flow into your heart. The Earth is not passive, though in contrast to the mind of reason it may seem that way. Only by allowing the heart to open into a fluid experience blended in an active embrace can we understand the vast range of lucid knowing that is here, waiting for us to remember.

It takes a while to develop a truly allowing mind that will accept and participate with this level of openness. You start by breaking habits, letting go of grasping and holding, and as energies no longer bound up in holding or fixating become available, you come more and more to the natural generosity of the indwelling openness of your heart.

Devotion

The Earth is an expression of the intent of the essence, arising as a support for all beings to return to origin. As you touch this unwavering reciprocal intent of Earth and the essence, you realize that everything is a teacher. A loving commitment and respect arise naturally as a profound trust in the essence and its countless manifestations. The devotion of the essence for all to return to origin is seen in the elemental equally loving commitment of gravity, air, soil, plants, water, fire, and space. The devotion arising in your heart for the Earth and the essence is also a reflection of the same intent guiding you through all appearances. This natural devotion gives the ability to bond and relate, to accept grace, to relinquish control and surrender.

True devotion is not obedience to a human authority or a hierarchy of doctrine. It is not meant to be a feudal obeisance. The mind plays a strong role in keeping you subject to the minds and ideas of others. If you let your mind become a tyrant, this sets up a willingness to delegate authority to external structures. You do not want to give away your responsibility, your ability to respond from your heart, to your mind or to another person. This does not mean that you do not have respect for spiritual guides. Your mind can still be an inner tyrant by refusing to listen to other voices besides the voice of your heart. You acknowledge your responsibility for your own journey and that the ultimate source of the path is the essence itself. You do not need to rely on human interpretation to meet the intent of the essence in your heart and all around you in the natural world. Devotion is about opening your heart to the soul of all that manifests naturally.

Humility

Giving yourself wholeheartedly, surrendering to the pull of the essence in your heart without any structure or any knowing how to do it, is humility. True humility is not submitting to a doctrine or following the rules. It is very subtle. It involves no new identity, no new status. You are empty, you give up yourself completely to the fabric of being as a blended acknowledgement outside hierarchy or achievement. The basic ground of spiritual practice is a feeling, a living wholeness; you just float in your humility, open and surrendering. When your mind steps out of the way and relinquishes control, you see clearly from your heart that you are already part of the oneness of the intent of the essence. As you allow the purpose of your heart to lead you, you simplify your life and bring your wants and needs down to nothing, and then all that comes to you is more than enough: it is a gift. This original way of being, respectful, and gentle, is the nurturing ground from which all spiritual growth arises.

Responding, allowing, devotion, and humility lead to an allowing mind that is open to the natural knowing in your heart, reverent and humble, touching and relating with the basis of this existence. But along with recognizing these qualities of the Earth within your heart, we cannot emphasize enough how living closer to the physical Earth, the actual ground of this life, knowing how to live and participate spiritually with our First Mother, is crucial to the path that brings us to the ultimate open luminous heart of inner radiance.

Letting Go

The Earth is the basic ground on which our lives and our spiritual practice evolve. It is the intent of the essence manifesting for all beings to seek and find the path of return to origin. This expression of the essence is like a dream, although it appears as if solid and real. All experience, all phenomena, are as evanescent as a mist in the midday sun, but this does not in any way diminish the inherent holiness of this manifest vision we call life. The whole of this wondrous world arises for us to follow the signs guiding, opening, and gentling us, helping us let go and surrender to the embrace of the essence. This vision of Earth is meant to be directly experienced, for us to feel the pulse of our Mother within and without, to make a deep connection with the attributes that are here for us to emulate. The expansiveness of sky, the fluidity of water, the perseverance of mountains, and the openness of Earth are here for us to witness, feel, touch, and experience with our whole being, so that they become alive within us and we recognize and accept our indwelling heritage.

To enter into the allowing openness of our hearts, we need to come into direct experience of the sacred nature of the Earth, the spontaneously arising vision of life within the fabric of being. When you begin to really feel and interact with the energies and blessings all around you, your heart will open naturally. To do this you need to break down the barriers that keep you separate from the natural world. After turning away from the Earth, our ancestors set up new cultural contexts, artificial constructs both physical and mental that reinforced separation from the Earth. Once these were in place, we held to and maintained them, and with that heritage of holding comes a fear that if whatever you are holding to breaks down, you will be lost.

For the most part, we have forgotten how to trust and embrace the Earth as our home. If you know the most basic survival skills, how to build a simple shelter of natural materials, how to make fire without flint or matches, how to find water and identify a few medicinal and edible plants, if you know how to live with our mother the Earth, you are no longer afraid on a most basic, primal level. This gives you a deep trust in the Earth and in yourself that allows the natural openness of your heart to unfold.

You do not have to become an expert in survival skills. The Earth skills for a spiritual life blended with the Earth are very simple, although they require letting go of many habits of mind and body. This is the greater part of the work for people raised in the modern world, as well as being a necessary aspect of the spiritual path at any time. Letting go of habits and experiencing the sacredness and generosity of the Earth will allow the indwelling openness of your heart to grow. The teachings surround you in the natural world. Let go into the stream of nature, enter into what you already have, a heart of joy ready to embrace and be embraced by the radiance of the essence. If your heart is open, you will be taught.

Earth Sitting

The Earth is the temple of the holy ones. If all the texts and written words were to disappear, you would still be surrounded and embraced by the teachings that are naturally present in this manifest world. So many of the spiritual metaphors that have come down to us in writing are based on direct expressions of the radiance of essence arising all around us. Openness is not like the sky, it is one with the sky, it is sky. Fluidity is not like water, it is one with the water, it is water. They are participatory, not conceptual. Wherever you are, the land itself is the actual basis of your spiritual practice. Listen to the voices of the winds, the waters, the rocks, the plants, the trees. They form the great song within which all other voices, human, bird, insect, and animal, are woven into a whole.

Go outdoors reverently, quietly, as if entering a shrine. Experience the wonders of this Earth with the innocence of a child. Sit for a while without expectations, watching cloud shapes billowing, growing, and spreading across the sky, and then dissolving into a blue expanse. Sit on a mountain, seeing mountain, feeling mountain, being mountain, entering into the strength of the rocks and trees. Sit with a pond or a small stream, feel the fluidity of water in motion and in stillness. Sit on a beach or a cliff above the sea, feel the depth and immensity of ocean as being. Sit on a hill looking out at an unobstructed blue sky or lie down and blend your whole being with the vastness overhead. Sit through the night waiting for the dawn or lie down on the Earth watching the stars pass over you. Witness the passage of the sun and moon and feel their movement within you.

Wherever you are, you can deepen your experience by keeping your body calm and relaxed. When walking, move slowly and quietly; when sitting, do not move after you have settled in. The most effective and traditional way to sit in openness and enter the subtle resonance of Earth and heart is to sit on the Earth, cross-legged, full lotus, half lotus, or in a more open cross-legged posture. If you are accustomed to any of these ways of sitting with only a small cushion or directly on the Earth, you can sit anywhere, at any time, and you do not need to bring a lot of equipment with you. The essential part of any posture is to keep your back upright but relaxed in its natural curves and your shoulders relaxed as well. Lift the upper part of your body slightly and root your lower body in the Earth. Feel the openness in the space between. This allows your subtle energy to move smoothly and helps you settle your mind and stay calm and alert. Your eyes are open but not focusing on anything in your field of vision. Breathe gently and evenly. Keep your chin tucked in a little bit and relax your jaw. Place the tip of your tongue to the roof of your mouth right behind your teeth to allow an even flow of the energies that arise while you practice. Relax into the posture, with a glimmer of a smile reflected in your eyes and mouth. This inner smile comes easily if you have a real appreciation for the hospitality of the spot you are sitting on, for its relatedness with you, the oneness of all life within the essence manifesting right here now. Once you have settled into the posture and the place do not move. Allow your subtle and physical energies to slow down.

Rest your speech in silence, and keep your breath soft and smooth, melting, blending, merging your responsiveness with the responsiveness of the Earth, not wandering off to the past or the future, but returning to whatever arises in your present experience. Keep your eyes from wandering also, settling your eyes gently, allowing the whole visual field all at once, until your eyes are sky-like, still, and vast. Your silence will blend with the space you have allowed, and your breath will slow and soften as if becoming the rhythmic pulse of a calm sea, the shallow even waves merging with the slope of the beach and elongating until the sound is hushed. If your being stirs and wanders then bring it back to this moment, peaceful and open, recognizing that you are part of the expansive vision unfolding around you.

Direct Perception

Direct perception is from the heart. We are born with the capacity for direct experience. Your heart is already waiting, like a small lamp deep in the woods, you can sense its warmth, and maybe see the glow up ahead. Your deepest heart will call to you if you are open to hearing its voice. All that separates us from our hearts are the elaborations created by our minds. Too often people experience the world secondhand with their perception clouded by a frenetic information overload. We as a species have allowed our intellect to take control and condemn or dismiss our hearts. Many people do not have any real sense of the value of the heart. We need to begin to break away from all the constraints of the mind, to move past the hold our minds have on our natural ability to perceive directly from the heart.

You may have had a brief glimpse of an aware openness that is beyond what you normally experience. Maybe it brought tears to your eyes and you prayed that you could re-experience it, perhaps by repeating it through your memory of how it happened originally, yet it does not come back. Direct perception arises organically, naturally. You must enter the heart of the vision that is this life, connect with it through your own heart, then experience the openings that this connection brings, openings into a world that is alive, arising, flowing, teaching you with its movement outside of words. Direct perception is a visionary world of experience opening up to you moment by moment out of the radiant intent of the essence. You begin to move and experience within a flow, a fluid ongoing sense of awakening guided by this call. It is in the sound of water, the morning light in the trees, the movement of grasses in the wind. Direct perception is this flow of being, a generative feeling blended with all feeling, the expression of the essence within you and within all that naturally arises. Direct perception is not the same as so-called objective observation by the mind. Direct perception is the true nature of experience revealed through the heart.

Wide-Angle Vision

Wide-angle vision is a powerful support for opening your heart as you sit or as you walk. Just as openness is the natural mode of your heart, wide-angle vision is the natural mode of your eyes. Original peoples used their eyes in wide-angle vision most of the time, using more tightly focused tunnel vision only for specific tasks. The modern world with its emphasis on the written word demands focused tunnel vision for most activities, and it has become a habit even when not necessary. This use of the eyes in turn reinforces tunnel mind, restricting and closing off access to other modes of perception. Learning to use the eyes in wide-angle vision, aware without focusing on the peripheral field, allows the mind to open to the natural spaciousness of the heart and eyes.

The mind or intellect is closely connected to the eyes; how you choose to use your eyes affects your mind. Wide-angle vision allows everything in a 180-degree range to come in all at once. This saturation of the visual field floods the brain with information and shifts attention to the receptive quality of the eyes, to receptiveness itself rather than content, softening the intensity of the mind and lessening its ability to control the heart. Wide-angle vision helps cut through the tendency of mind or intellect to take over, and you can settle more easily into your heart. And because it is the natural way to use our eyes, this is a very effective way for spiritual practitioners to reclaim direct experience of the natural indwelling openness of our hearts and reconnect with the fabric of being.

Most people have allowed their minds to be dominant and use their eyes in a channeled, tunnel vision way, not only through habitually focusing on the written word, but also by grabbing blindly out of the negative emotions and limitations of separate identity upheld by the mind. This experience of the mind can be very compelling, making it difficult to access the natural inclusiveness and openness of your heart. Wide-angle vision can help release the hold that the mind has on the eyes and on the heart. The eyes go naturally into wide-angle vision when you go to your heart, and the process is reciprocal; intentionally going into wide-angle vision facilitates blending with your heart and the heart of all.

Earth Walking

Find a natural area or a trail that is private, and walk very, very slowly and quietly. The point is not to concentrate on going slow, but to allow the slowness to open all your senses, to expand your perception rather than tunneling in. Use your feet to slow yourself down. Walk barefoot or in flexible thin-soled shoes with little or no heel, feeling the Earth meet your foot at each step. In the ancient way of Earth walking, you shift out of the headlong heel-first movements of our contemporary rushing world into the more respectful, balanced cadence of walking as a prayer of openness feeling the pulse of life all around you. Placing each foot gently, slowly, you touch the ground first with the outside of the ball of your foot, then roll the ball toward your instep. Then place the heel, then the toes, not placing your full weight until you really feel the ground beneath your foot for any twigs, leaves, or pebbles there. This frees your movements from reliance on your eyes; you sense the ground with your feet instead. This receptive way of walking helps you to slow down and walk very quietly, blending with the life around you.

Allow all your movements to be fluid and graceful. It may seem awkward at first, but as the rhythms of this way of walking become more natural for you, you will move more and more like ripples across still water, melting effortlessly into the whole. With your sight resting lightly on the horizon ahead of you, keep your eyes in wide-angle vision, aware without focusing on whatever appears at the edge of your field of vision. As you walk in this way with wide-angle vision, the world seems more fluid, moving with you, and the naturally molten quality of all experience becomes more evident.

Slow walking in wide-angle vision shifts ordinary patterns of motion and time and allows entrance into a more expansive sense of openness. It will also connect you to subtle perceptions not only of the physical world but of the spirit world as well, and as you become more in tune with the heartbeat of the Earth, the dividing line between the physical and the spiritual will dissolve. Especially when you do this practice at night, it will intensify your awareness of the good and bad energies of the different areas you are moving through, giving you an inner experience of the spirit energies that can linger on the land, a valuable knowing for living within this shared vision.

Waiting for Animals

Sit in an area that feels good and inviting, calm your body and mind, and wait for animals. When you go for a walk, pay attention to the movements of animals, follow the patterns of birds, learn the activities of insects and fish, then find a spot nearby where you can be close to their rhythms, using the whole experience to settle into your heart, with a knowing in your silent presence that you are part of this arising vision. Once you have settled in, the animals, birds, and insects will slowly resume their natural flow of activity all around you. It takes time for both you and the animals to calm down. Almost everyone has felt the blessing in the unexpected approach of a large or small free animal or bird, and the spontaneous openness, respect, and gratitude for the gift of this trust. When animals come close to you, still your beating heart and soften your tightening breath so you do not scare them away. Stay with openness and gratitude, keeping your eyes in wide-angle vision. Animals will feel the focus of your eyes, and your energy will be reflected in the way they act around you.

Sitting and waiting quietly for animals, keeping your eyes in wide-angle vision as an animal comes closer, is good training for recognizing the power of your eyes and how you are using them. Just as animals will feel the quality of your eyes, you will feel the quality of their eyes as well. Animals can also reach out with their eyes, and they are very sensitive to this use. They will bolt if your eyes grab onto to them in an ordinary way. Training in wide-angle vision while waiting for animals helps develop reverent eyes that connect naturally with the allowing openness of your heart. Waiting for animals is a profound training for your whole being; it is a practice of opening to the approach of grace, and the skills you develop in this way are vital for the spiritual path and especially for the visionary path of radiance, which is a practice of the approach of grace in a very pure form.

In addition to providing a focal point for calming your mind and body and settling into your heart, waiting for animals allows you to experience the interrelatedness of all life in a very direct way. Once you have settled into a spot, and the animals, birds, and insects around you have resumed their own rhythms, you can witness countless subtle interactions. A hawk calls, a small animal holds very still. A butterfly glides through a patch of sunlight, a deer steps out into the open in the same clearing. They are all taking cues from each other, weaving patterns of caution and ease. Like concentric rings expanding outward on the surface of water, the echoes of their actions constantly radiate and intertwine. You feel firsthand the truly dynamic quality of the oneness of all beings as manifestations of the same essence and the same life of the Earth. We are all born of the same mother. We are all brothers and sisters, literally. Communication is ongoing and seamless. Whether we hear them or not, the voices of our relatives are everywhere. The personal lives of animals unfolding around you are reflections within the radiant intent of the essence, and in the intricate beauty of a flower or the rippling music of a mountain stream, you touch other expressions of that sacred intent that permeates the fabric of being embracing all.

Good Spots Bad Spots

Tranquil and dynamic energies are an integral part of all that naturally arises. As you settle into the feelings and rhythms of the Earth with your heart, you will be more sensitive to positive and negative energies in the areas that you come across. You may feel that some places have a special responsive quality, while others may seem hostile. These are not random energies. The circumstances for their arising may sometimes involve human activity, but areas may also have a deep-seated tone within the fabric of the Earth that has drawn other positive or negative experiences to that spot.

In any given area, there will be specific feelings that speak to you. It is best to focus on positive sites that are willing to provide beneficial energy and circumstances for your practice. A good spot that you have approached respectfully and that is welcoming you is an invitation for a union of intent. But some spots, although they may look sublime and welcoming, may turn out to be the opposite. When practicing in such areas, you might find your mind becoming increasingly agitated, turning toward negative thoughts or extreme emotions, when just a few moments before you were at peace.

Wherever you go, pay attention to what the land is telling you. If you choose to sit, once you have settled

into a spot, notice how you feel. If you begin to feel
unusually restless, uneasy, edgy, or disturbed, you may
want to get up and go somewhere else. Be aware of
where this feeling is coming from. Has the spot
reminded you of an argument you have had, or a
personal fear, or are you feeling the residues of other
beings' arguments or fears left there? Perhaps you are
feeling the place itself, or the territorial warnings from
an anthill or a bird's nest nearby, or perhaps a spirit,
good, bad, or neutral, lives there. It is important to
read the energy of an area accurately so that you can
choose the energy you want to be with. Even on a
good spot, your mind may bring up its own
negativities. You need to look honestly at the feelings
arising from within and around you and be able to
distinguish them. All experiences are teachers,
supplying valuable information for the wordless
knowing in your body and heart that will help guide
you in the future.

Later as your practice of Earth sitting deepens, you
may choose to experience bad spots intentionally, to
enrich and strengthen your resolve toward an open
heart as a prayer for all life, a prayer for all beings to
recognize their original heart. It is important to have a
purpose vast in scope, outside of self, at all times, and
especially when you are practicing with a negative spot.
This practice is also best done with a group at first or
with an experienced guide.

A Heart Place

For people who hold heavy emotions or deep burdens from past lives, or scars from intense experiences that happened in childhood or later, you need to find an especially good spot in nature that you feel a strong connection with, a place that responds to you and wants to help you, a place that makes you feel safe, secure, and comforted, a mother energy, a heart place. You do not need the forceful energies of a shaman spot or the challenges of a negative spot.

Many people in modern cultures have issues with their mothers in this life, in part because these cultures do not support nurturing mothering energies in general and consider them of lesser value. The Earth is outside those constraints and offers nurturing freely. Everyone needs a place to connect with this nurturing energy in times that are particularly trying, intense, and challenging. You need to feel the landscape and know in your heart the kind of qualities that are there. You need to feel totally safe, protected, and nurtured. You need the loving, embracing, reliable, comforting, unconditional acceptance that the Earth can give you.

Whatever heavy burden you are carrying, just sit down in wide-angle vision and thankfulness and let the Earth absorb the weight of your emotions and memories, or the leaden burdens of past lives. You do not have to think about them, or work through a psychological process, or direct a flow of energy. You do not have to push the heaviness away, just let the weight of it sink, let the grace of gravity absorb the heaviness. Just sit and give yourself and your burden to the Earth. A heart place connects your heart directly to the heartbeat of the essence manifesting as the Earth. The natural brightness at your heart is like a small candle flame touching another larger flame as you sit with the Earth on a heart place. As the shadow of the burden falls away, you feel the warmth and light at your heart that is naturally there and feel it embraced by the larger warmth and light of the Earth.

This may take some time if your burden is long held, but if you sit repeatedly with a heart place it will slowly be absorbed, and you will be able to let go of more and more of the weight. Difficult memories will not completely fade away, but the deep holding will slowly be released. A heart place is an upwelling of love that will dissolve the burden you are releasing, freeing the indwelling love and nurturing already in your heart to radiate out to others, and as your caring extends beyond yourself, the heaviness and holding will fade away even more.

Blindfolded Walking

Earth walking blindfold outdoors, within the slow soft rhythms of the Earth, is a beautiful way to quiet your mind and open your heart. Without the boundaries maintained by your eyes, you perceive the world in a very different way. You can walk following a string that you touch lightly, or on a trail that is obvious in a tactile way to your feet, or with tall grass or thick underbrush on either side, whatever you need to feel confident of your route. Any side trails can be closed off with string. You want an area and a route that feel safe to you so that you can move freely, surrendering to the flowing movements of the slow walk, surrendering to the timelessness hidden behind ordinary perception.

Normally, we hold strongly to our sense of the outer world with our eyes. The way things look, solid and real, distant or near, are all upheld by the way the brain reads the information from our eyes. The eyes connect with both voluntary and involuntary nervous systems, so how you use your eyes affects your responses to your experience on many levels. You can loosen the hold that the mind has on your perceptions by blindfolding and allowing other senses to open out. You begin to perceive light directly without using your eyes. You become more aware of the presence of trees, bushes, and the space around you. Stay in wide-angle vision behind the blindfold. Even though you are not seeing directly with the eyes, it is important to maintain a connection to that quality of openness. You may experience a sense of knowing exactly where the trail is. Some people may see in their inner eye a path that glows, and other people may just know in their hearts that they are going in the right direction.

For this deepening of experience, allow yourself several hours at a time to do the practice. Walking blindfold, moving so slowly, shuts down all concepts of motion. Flowing and continuous, with no coming or going, no here or there, you become one with your experience arising moment by moment. Eventually, after several hours of moving in this non-moving way, you can take off your blindfold and keeping your eyes in wide-angle vision, continue to allow yourself along the trail, vast as space, a knowing that is form in movement, nothing more.

Hunting Your Heart

All the avenues we offer are ways of bringing spiritual practice back to its origins, back to heart and Earth. They are doorways for coming to original heart naturally in the course of your experience, and a crucial element for allowing original heart to unfold is that your mind has to get out of the way. Habits of mind and concepts do not just magically disappear, you have to want to let them go, you have to want to not be fenced in by them. The spiritual path at any stage is an ongoing process of letting go, and whether in retreat or in the context of other aspects of your life, this requires that you change all your habits, how you respond to your experience on many levels.

You need to get all the concepts and labels out of the way, all the judgments and comparisons, all "this is like that." Relating a new experience to something you already know could be a stepping-stone, a way to establish trust, permission granted by yourself from inside to go in an unfamiliar direction, or too often "just like that" becomes another brick in the wall of your certainty, the circumscribed space of what you already know. True spiritual practice is about openness and direct experience, clearly perceived, unexpected, fresh, aware, moment by moment, not empty, not absent, but fully present, open like the air, fluid like clear water, blending your heart with the heart of all.

Hunting your heart moves you beyond the barriers of the circumscribed space of what you already know, to reveal an openness and fluidity in the natural world and in your heart in ways that will bring you to directly experience the heart and the heart of all. We all walk, we all move, everyday. How you move is already part of your path. One way of hunting your heart is using a very, very slow form of Earth walking combined with standing and sitting all within a flow, a blended openness, letting the landscape and the day play you like music, moving with the wind, moving with the shadows and the light, moving quietly, slowly, pausing at times, no ripples from your movements, no ripples from your mind, your feet and heart connecting with the Earth at each step.

Most people in our fast paced contemporary culture let their minds play their movements, walking in response to their thoughts, often about places or times other than where they are, or if in the present, monitoring the experience, judging good or bad, or hurrying on a trail to get to an overlook up ahead, missing the relational experience that is all around us at every moment. You need to literally step out of your mind to really be in your heart, entering a relational openness with every step along the trail.

Breaking Habits

In order to let go fully, opening to your senses, opening to your heart, you need to break habits of personal identity as well as habits of perception and movement. We are all accustomed to certain ways of being, certain routes we take, certain ways of doing things in our daily lives, and over time they become restrictive, inhibiting us and blinding us to our hearts. Habits can help some aspects of life go more smoothly, but the lack of attention fostered by routines and the accompanying false sense of the stability of objects, situations, and times covers over the freshness and immediacy through which the intent of essence is most clearly seen shining within its expressions.

To go beyond habitual tendencies you need to want to let them go. You can start by letting go of little things. Choose an activity you do every day, such as brushing your teeth with your right hand, or putting your left shoe on first, and then do the opposite. Breaking a habit in this way may be awkward or humorous at first, but over time, it will become automatic. At this point, drop the new habit and go back to your original way of doing things, then pick another habit to change. Gradually choose larger and larger habits. Do this over a period of years. Though the changes may seem curious and whimsical at first, if you persist, they bring about a very subtle but profound shift in your way of being. You are making an end run around your mind. You begin to see through all habits and patterns of holding, and you are not so bound by them, which engenders a new kind of freedom. Letting go of habits willingly or playfully gives you a confidence in your ability to change. You will be lighter and freer, like ice returning to water. No longer fixed and rigid, becoming fluid and flexible, you will be less compelled by the story of your identity, "I always," "I never," and so forth. The categories of who you think you are lose their intensity and the habit of self and its demands have less effect on you.

Heading into times of great change it is very helpful to shift habits voluntarily before they are shifted for you. It makes it easier to cope with big changes in a constructive and creative way if you are not held down by your habits, by how things ought to be. This is most easily seen in accounts of people finding themselves in survival situations where they have lost all their habitual routines and supports and feel they have nothing to rely on. Disorientation from the sudden loss of habits is an added burden to what is already a life and death situation. You are far better able to cope and survive if you know how to live within the natural world with a fluid and open heart, able to calmly recognize all that is offered to you rather than be overcome by fear, seeing only what you do not have.

Night Sit

To sit through the night on a good spot and wait for the dawn can pull you out of your habitual world very directly by plunging you into the night's presence. Sitting alone within the immensity and the darkness of the night, you are faced with the depth of the unknowable. Boundaries fall away, you are aware of the frailty of your existence. Starlight touches you with the vast distances of space. Moonlight softens all details, turning the familiar landmarks of your world into fragile shells of shadow and pale light. Surrendering to the silence and darkness of the night, you merge with a vastness delicate and ephemeral as star shine, seamless as the night itself mirroring the depth of the essence beyond radiance.

The night covers over so much of what we habitually experience through light, but the sense of hearing, the tactile knowing of skin, and inner experience of the heart are all enhanced. You are more sensitive to the energies in the area where you are sitting, not only of the land itself and the plants, but also the feelings of the beings moving within the landscape, the animals of the night and the shades of tensions wandering on their desires.

Sitting with the night opens your mind beyond your ordinary perceptions and expands into a deeper experience of your heart touching a livingness all around you that becomes palpable. Even the darkness is alive. As you wait within the silent presence of the night, shedding all that blinds you to this expanded vision, remaining with the night, your heart opens like a prayer flowing over the Earth. Blending with the night, motivated by your purpose for all beings to acknowledge the essence within themselves, you can touch the stars in your heart. Your mind will let go as your heart expands more and more, just as the dawn will surely come.

Death

Any time you sit alone, and particularly in the night, you may come to feel the presence of your inevitable death. Everything that manifests passes away again in an ongoing process. Each moment, each breath, encompasses whole worlds, whole cycles of creation and dissolution. Death is a constant companion; death is part of any change. Acceptance on a deep level of the natural presence of death allows the entire range of energies and life processes to move more freely, allows you to meet the essence more directly in your experience. Acknowledging death gives you an ability to accept loss and grief as part of the creative process of life. You will not get stuck in the frustration of holding to lost loved ones or lost opportunities in the past, and you will be more open to new situations, not afraid of where they will lead or if they will last. A genuine feeling that your own death can come at any moment can heighten your livingness now.

Death is an active agent in the cycle of life. Birth, growth, maturity, and death are all part of how the intent of essence manifests and how you learn, how you do anything in this world. The problems and fears that come up are due to denial of the basic underlying dynamics of this experience. Decline into death is universal, and how you feel about death is an indicator of how you relate to the changes of transformation woven throughout the fabric of being. Access this feeling, this poignant, ephemeral aspect of all life; touch it within your whole being, then the self-important mind that deals in certainties will let go of its hold over your heart. Mind will no longer be the controlling factor in your life, and its role will diminish to its natural function as a simple tool to be used when needed.

As mind relinquishes its hold, this will also help undermine concepts of personal permanence. When you solidify your experience and become cut off from the ephemeral arising nature of life and the lessons that it offers, there is a corresponding feeling that you have plenty of time that dulls the sense of urgency you need for the spiritual path. Death is a true friend. Sitting with the night and your inevitable death clarifies your relationship to the intent of the essence and the purpose in your heart, helps you touch the intent at the core of your very being, teaching your mind to stand down and allow the heart to flourish.

Simplifying Your Life

All beings have habitual patterns, and humans not only have personal patterns but complex cultural patterns as well. Many of these larger patterns are revealing themselves to be very destructive to the Earth. As you develop momentum for changing habits you may also want to consider making larger changes in how you live, cutting back on or disengaging from some modern practices such as electrical power, petroleum products, defecating in water, chemical agriculture, GMO, processed, or packaged foods, technologies based on rare earths, and so forth, out of respect for our Mother. These changes may come naturally, as renunciation grows within you, or they may be in relation to breaking habits and an awareness of death, but no matter how you come to them, they are potent and much needed actions. How you relate with the Earth is reflected in your spiritual path. Your choices at any level, from how you eat and live to your deepest beliefs, affect your spiritual growth.

Graceful or difficult, your whole life, the sum of all your choices and perceptions, is already a spiritual path. You can choose to further complicate your life and accumulate more elaborations including those of the mind, or you can simplify to better hear the primordial voice of grace reflected in the heart of all life.

In our contemporary world of accelerating mental complexity, the underlying ground of our experience is often obscured. Original heart, the radiant breath of the fabric of being is not reached through conceptual systems, but through direct experience. This aware presence as it shines out moment by moment from within the arising vision we call life is not accessed through elaboration, but through simplifying your life to be open to the subtlety of its call.

For many people on a spiritual path this is a reason to seek time apart in retreat, and you may find yourself in a formal retreat setting at some point in your journey, but the real work of spiritual growth does not start there. The momentum of all your experience up to the moment you enter retreat is an integral part of the process of retreat, and has a great deal to do with why you are there and whether you stay even through the hard parts. True retreat begins long before you enter a cloistered space in time for any kind of spiritual practice. The spiritual path is a life's journey, and simplifying your life allows a space for the heart of all being to be heard so you can follow this call to a blended experience, returning to the natural state, our birthright, our primordial way of being.

Renunciation

True renunciation is not something you force yourself to do. It comes of itself, after years and years of letting go of attachments to habits and emotions and recognizing the connection between yourself and the essence. Letting go cuts through aspects of life that you take for granted, and over the years, you find the space that was once filled by habits and elaborations is now open and free. You feel more sense of connection with all life, less separation, more openness; there is less in the way. Slowly you begin to let go of bigger chunks of habitual tendencies. You walk away from them easily, smoothly, without looking back. This renunciation is a way of being, not a static state; it is an ongoing motion of letting go that arises out of your heart once you have begun to polish your personal sphere of experience. It comes naturally out of the joy within this grand vision arising to fulfill its own reflection, with an openness and fluidity that allows more and more space within which spiritual awareness can grow and be felt and experienced. And as more habits of mind are dropped aside, you are filled in return by the growing responsiveness of your heart.

As openness and fluidity grow stronger, be careful not to weaken your experience by putting it into words too soon, either to yourself or to others. This is not about keeping secrets but about honoring the new within and allowing your heart the space to grow and blossom without being shaped or stunted by words and concepts. It is about letting go of the need to reinforce identity or solidify the process of change with new stories of becoming. Spiritual growth is an art; you are letting a new dimension of your spiritual life unfold. It is like being in a studio, allowing a piece of artwork to gestate in its own way. If you reach a point at which you really need to speak about your experience or spiritual life, speak with a true guide with whom you have a deep heart connection, or go outside to a heart place and talk with the Earth, talk with a tree; they know about patience and slow steady growth, they know the silence of strong roots.

Giving

Along with letting go of habits, letting go of possessions and giving them to others is a wonderful way to support and energize your spiritual life. The size or amount does not matter; it could be a small portion of your lunch offered to a sparrow, but this giving, however simple, can profoundly open you. Whenever we were about to move or make a change in our lives, we gave things away. Even when we had few belongings, we still made offerings of them when we moved. Our giving was not only a prayer for spiritual growth, but also a prayer for the harmony of all life, a prayer of thankfulness for this entire unfolding sacred vision, for the beauty around us and the chance to follow the lessons being imparted to us at every step of this journey. The giving and the gratitude lightened our load, opened our hearts and made our path clearer.

In our extremely materialistic culture, people are too often possessed by what they think they own. They belong to their belongings and identify themselves through them. There is no real ownership; things are only temporarily with us. When we let go of the burden of possession, the lie of ownership, we open ourselves to the possibility of entering a wider belonging, becoming part of the greater unowned and unownable wholeness suffusing all. The offerings and the thanks given are stepping-stones to oneness; every step deepens your experience, opening your heart to the universe. Offer your heart and give thanks to this entire sacred arising expression of the essence, the glory and the grace that is naturally present and always abiding. Giving is a prayer for this grace to continue guiding, confronting, and teaching you at every step. Make offerings to the wind rippling in the grass, prayers to the land, give thanks to the sky that you may open to the vast teachings before you, aligning your heart with the generosity of the intent of the essence.

Opening Your Heart

In all these practices of letting go, there is a sense of stepping outside ordinary parameters and perceptions and becoming aware of a much wider view, a view that cannot be nailed down or defined in specific terms and can only be felt and experienced in an allowing way. This is the realm of the heart. Original peoples naturally locate knowing in their hearts, as in the eloquent hand gesture sweeping out from the heart to indicate understanding in Native American sign language. Many peoples of the Earth have recognized the heart as the center of true knowing. Relying on the wisdom of your heart is to accept our indwelling heritage of natural connection with the heart of all being.

Realm of the Heart

The heart quality is unbounded, outside judgments or comparisons and is not separate from the vision we call this life. It is a natural doorway to original heart. Your heart knows how to respond to the expansiveness of the blue sky because we are all one within this vision, we are part of it, an integral love. The oneness that is here now all around us is felt directly in the heart. The energy of the heart is like water, it connects, there is no separation. In any body of water, whether river, pond, lake, or ocean, each molecule of water is joined to every other molecule of water so that they are essentially one molecule. And like water, the seamless fluidity of the heart is extremely responsive to the fluidity within the fabric of being. We are already seamless with all life; we need only recognize it.

Feelings radiating out from each being touch all other beings, they have an effect. The heart is not neutral; it is engaged. A great deal of stress in contemporary human social interaction is due to the effort of denying our feelings or the feelings we are receiving from others. But feelings are valuable. Love, compassion, appreciation, and thankfulness are the true actions of the heart. These feelings are pathways to the expansive knowing that encompasses more than words and concepts. Feeling thankful for every aspect of this great arising vision opens your heart. True caring, true love, true gratitude are powerful forces; they can move worlds, they can move you to fruition.

Some people have shadowed places in their hearts, something that happened in the past either in childhood or in adulthood, a hurt. For some it is lodged in the heart as a black spot or a pain or a numbness, and they shy away from it. The simplest most effective way to move directly past those places and access the natural expansiveness of the heart is to sit with the Earth on a good spot, a heart place. As you sit, you can also focus on breathing in and out through your heart for a few moments or longer, and then bring up strong feelings of love or appreciation. The effectiveness comes from being in your heart with the Earth, not from visualizing or imagining but really feeling centered in your heart, really feeling love, really feeling appreciation, really feeling the tangible reciprocity the Earth is offering to you at that spot. The breathing is a support and a way in, the love and appreciation and your relationship with the Earth are essential. You can do this as a practice; it will melt through the pain. Gradually you will be able to sustain the feelings of love and send them out to others, expanding your sphere of loving, merging with the nurturing energy of the Earth and encompassing all beings, all life.

Realm of the Intellect

In our contemporary world, a vast majority of people are lost in linear mind, the intellect afflicted by and enamored of its elaborations and certainties, and separated from the heart. There are also many people doing spiritual practice who have been practicing for years who are locked in this mind and have not let go of the world it has created.

The mind of the intellect is opaque, dense, insular, and self-seduced. It cannot see outside its own view. It remains trapped in a hall of mirrors, ensnared in its own complexities and disconnected from direct perception, taking its interpretations of experience to be real. This reaches an apex in the philosophies in which all experience is held to be only a projection of mind, a further expression of the mind's self-absorption. Even without a formal philosophical stance, the mind is still lost in the fantasy it considers reality, distanced neurologically by a thirty second delay on all incoming sensory information and insulated by a continuous internal overlay to mask the thirty seconds, the reflexive "I knew that," which obscures the gap and assures the mind that it knew all along. It is literally, continuously, out of touch and has created a worldview that sees only itself, judging everything by its own criteria and discounting anything that does not fit, resulting in our contemporary mind so lost in its elaborations that it has forgotten the ability to listen to the heart. The intellect should be a support for the heart wisdom expressing itself. Instead, the intellect has gone beyond its natural function. It has taken over and become virulent, a parasite that no longer cares if it kills its host.

As agrarian cultures arose and became increasingly separated from the more fluid ungoverned rhythms of natural life, the mind divided the natural flow of being into sacred and profane. Spiritual experience became enshrined in special structures that mimicked the qualities of the natural world. The instinctive demand in the hearts of mystics throughout time to go deeper into the wilderness to make direct connection with the indwelling sacredness of all life was exploited and relegated to temples consecrated not as part of the seamless continuity of life but as something other, a constructed image of the natural world, and often, monuments to power.

Special places separate from nature but intended to reflect the spiritual experience, the soaring shapes of cathedrals, temples, and mosques evoked the presence of great trees in the forest and the vault of the sky, and later stained glass windows mimicked the inner radiance of rainbow light. Many religious structures are molded out of trees and stones into imitations of nature. Using materials taken from what naturally arises to reinforce ideas of separation from that arising also reinforced the idea that doctrine and authority were superior to direct experience in the wilderness. The natural world became suspect, something to be controlled and kept at bay. The Earth and nature, now profane, were seen as alien and dangerous.

The rise of agriculture and the structures that arose with it had far-reaching repercussions on how we perceive our world and ourselves. Natural movement within cyclical time became linear history, life imprisoned in a line, a spiraling line at best, held between two points, suspended between here and there, before and after. We lost the inclusive encompassing dimensions of the eternal present and the heart. Instead of moving through time and space with the wide-angle view of the heart, open to subtle ever-changing shifts in the environment all around us, we began to attempt to own and control our world, clearing land and cultivating only certain plants. We set those plants in rows, channeled the natural life of the waters, and exiled plants that would not or did not serve our needs.

No longer moving within grace and change, we sought fixed conditions in soils and crop yields, in weather and water supplies, and in our own minds. Religions arose that offered magic powers and acted as agents for consolidating wealth and resources in the hands of an elite few, the emerging ruling class. Spiritual experience, no longer a matter of openness and clear perception of direct experience, was eclipsed by a need to impose patterns and certainties, subsumed in rituals to support our efforts to control each other and control and reshape our world. We sought structure and stability and became suspicious of fluidity and change. Rows and rows of identical crops required identical circumstances to be repeated reliably with no alien weeds. Rains had to come at the right time, but not too much and never during harvest. Tunnel mind arose with early cultivation through a need to focus, repeat, and impose a specific pattern of one-way interaction on a naturally fluid interactive world. Rhythms informing life were no longer those of acceptance of grace and openness to the unexpected, but those of exclusion and demand. We isolated ourselves from life and in so doing, we isolated ourselves from the natural rhythms of our hearts and their resonate fields.

Rather than living and moving within the sacredness of origin, we tried to become petty gods, rulers over our own small plots carved out of a generous all. Ownership, hierarchy, status, and doctrine, calibrating with the mind, replaced feeling from the heart and its wider scope of nuance. We have been drugged by the magic spell of the power of the intellect for so long that we take it to be human nature when in fact it is not. There are many ways to perceive and communicate outside the neural pathways of the brain. Electromagnetic energies move efficiently and swiftly throughout the galaxies, measurable in the background radiation of the universe, the signature of the cyclic nature of the cosmos, and in the heartbeats of the Earth and the tiniest insect. The heart is the most powerful generator of electromagnetic energy in our bodies, producing far more electromagnetic energy than the brain. The brain will naturally follow the heart and the Earth if we are centered in the heart instead of in our heads. The resonant frequency of our mother planet Earth is 7.83 Hz, a frequency associated with alpha waves for creativity and healing. The choice to become aware again from the natural seat of our souls to heal and restore the original relationship of mind and heart literally puts you back in touch with the heart of the Earth.

And ironically, at this time on the Earth, as natural resources are being depleted or destroyed at an accelerating rate, one of the ways to realign with our First Mother's frequency and heal is to grow a garden. Planting and tending a garden offers a way to bridge the widening gap between our lives and the heart of the Earth. Gardening with respectful openness to the natural processes and cycles of plants and soil, as in Masanobu Fukuoka's way of natural farming, can connect us in a very direct way with the generosity and wisdom of the Earth and help us resanctify our most basic relationship with life. Gardening as a reciprocal act of cooperation can help heal the severance between daily and spiritual life, and support a path of freeing the heart from the cultivation of the mind.

Heartfulness and Mindfulness

In a culture dominated by the intellect, setting your mind to watch or investigate itself can be tricky. The mind is an obstacle when you let it lead, when you let it focus on itself.

The heart is the seat of spiritual growth, the place of direct experience, the true vantage point, the true view, the doorway to the blended fluid maturing inherent to all life. The practices of the heart involve a natural openness, a relatedness that is nurturing and whole. Heartfulness is not the same process as using your mind to watch itself or to watch you do something. To go through a day of mindfulness checking and rechecking your practice, keeping careful account from the place of the mind, shuts down your connection with your heart. This leads to an intellectual idea or concept of spiritual progress that is a creation of the mind, a built structure of openness, the vault of a cathedral rather than the sky.

Heartfulness is a different process, a process of letting go into openness and allowing the heart to be the basis of your experience. All you must do is return to your heart, at all times. It is here that you move closer to the natural state, original heart, the heart breath of the fabric of being. The Earth is all heart, and so going into a wilderness or any natural environment while being in wide-angle vision and

Earth walking is extremely helpful and brings you to your heart without the burden of concepts, ideas, and doctrine, through blending your heart with the heart of the Earth and all that manifests naturally from the essence. The radiant intent of the essence is the heart. Go to your heart as a way of being, not as a construct of the mind. Blend with the vision that is this life and become a part of the heartfulness of all being.

Reentering Your Heart

Many of us are brought up and educated in a way that creates the common error of thinking our feeling, our knowing, and our spiritual practice. Many have become so indoctrinated and habituated to this mode that they have no genuine experience, awareness, or memory of any other. Too often, sadness and grief are the only doorways left to the heart, and they are often denied or repressed. Sadness and grief can be powerful openings to allow another way of experiencing to arise. They offer a gap that allows a new form of perception to flower, although many people shy away from the pain. This distancing upon distancing has led to the many disturbing events in our world that further reinforce the reflex to close down emotionally and view the world by remote through intellectualization. It is important for authentic living and spiritual growth to be able to distinguish between the filtered experience of the intellect and direct experience of the heart.

The heart speaks through images that arise fluidly, organically, inseparable from feelings and a wordless knowing. This becomes clearer the more you embrace the Earth within your heart. The intellect uses words and can visualize, but its images are different, often crystalline in quality and constructed of details based on concepts and ideas of value and ranking rather than intuitive feeling. You need to recognize the difference between the labels, concepts, and judgments of the mind and the more open, inclusive, embraced perceptions of your heart as they speak to you. In whatever you do, you must be aware of the mind from the heart's perspective and see how the mind can hold and grasp on to anything, creating barriers instead of openings. Pay attention to what your feelings and your senses are telling you outside of words. We need to reenter our hearts and begin feeling again, no matter how painful at first, to reclaim direct experience and response.

Outside the ordinary ways of perceiving that stifle the quality of heart, we enter the space of generous knowing that is oceanic yet simple, vast yet personal. We begin to perceive an openness that has no boundaries, a natural knowing, a receptive humble embrace as one touches, communicates with, and is taught by the radiance of origin in all its myriad forms, from the cells in our bodies, dewdrops in the grass, the touch of a hand, the sounding of the stars in the night sky. True openness is reciprocal. We are not alone, we live within a dynamic interactive aware universe, a dance of perceptions that meet and interact with the countless other perceptions of countless other lives. Our minds may believe they are alone in a world of projections, but we are not. We are woven as one heart strand of living light within the fabric of all life. This is original heart.

Letting Go of the Knower

The knower is one of the more easily recognizable tactics of the mind to maintain control, and once you become aware of it from a heart's perspective, you can begin to break down the walls that it has held in place limiting and confining your experience. Letting go of the knower is crucial to the spiritual path, you cannot come to original heart with a mind that dictates, "I know." You need to come to original heart fresh each time, clear like light on water, unimpeded by the mind, unimpeded by the knower. The knower goes away slowly as you let go of the need for certainties, as you let go of the need to know. And as the knower dissolves away, the mind becomes allowing and deeper and deeper aspects of the heart arise within you.

You need to be aware of the knower and the reflex to feel that you know, and you need to have a decisive intent to be rid of it, a heartfelt recognition that the knower stands between you and a true ability to progress along the path. People can develop a knower around anything, especially spiritual practice: spirit walking, sacred Earth skills, knowing key points of practice or doctrine, helping people, healing people. You have to let go of whatever you think you know without having a new certainty to replace it. The point is not to be the best person at letting go but to be able to come to your experience totally fresh each time; this is what original heart is about, this is what the vision that is this life is about, utterly fresh in every moment, beyond the knower.

Relinquishing the knower requires that your mind surrender to not knowing, and is willing to experience your heart and your life from that openness. It is not surrendering to a doctrine or a system of belief, not surrendering to a new certainty, a new "I know that," but surrendering to the not knowing itself, spacious, clear, aware, no holding, fluid and humble. You need the humbleness of the Earth to let go of the knower, to meet the unknown, to let go of the tendency to grab onto new certainties.

The reflex to grab onto certainty is everywhere. We saw it in the art world, at the wilderness school, and in followers of various paths of spiritual practice. People holding to a knower just end up with another thing they know. It takes humbleness and courage, and an intensity of purpose from the heart, to be able to experience the world from the unknown, from the place of not knowing, open, connected, clear and aware, a lucid sense of being within a larger flow of intent every moment of every day, moving within a path of life as vision unfolding moment by moment.

You are leaving the realm of rigidity and entering a flowing expanse. One is stasis, and the other is a spontaneous flow of openness that gives rise to the fluid aware knowing of your heart. The knower is an experience within the mind, opaque and fixed, connected only to itself. Not knowing is when your mind stands down and allows your heart to open into its own knowing. The knowing in your heart is a different kind of knowing, connected to everything, flowing, clear, expansive, and relational, arising within you and all around you, a natural aware touch of the larger knowing, the sacred intent moving you toward the acknowledgement of original heart on the path to origin.

Courage

The fluid knowing from the heart, blended with the heart of all manifestation outside concepts and doctrine, is the natural way for us to express our lives. This is a knowing that is a tone from origin, the source. It is felt in the heart, as the heart, and here lies courage, the courage to live a heart's path in the face of a pervasive view that endlessly promotes the perspective of the mind, a worldview that is destroying the heart of this Earth.

Now more than ever it takes great courage to live clearly and directly from the heart. The mind has gone unchallenged and has become increasingly authoritarian as it has extended its reach, and it has even taken for itself and intellectualized positive qualities that are the province of the heart. Even without the distortions and interferences of the mind, life naturally offers a full range of experience. The challenge is to stay within the openness of the heart, stay with the seat of courage, your connection with all life. Your relationship with your mind is not just a private affair: it affects all life around you. The courage to stand up to the dominance of the mind and follow your heart is on behalf of all being: it is honoring the generous heart of all.

The Intent Within Your Heart

Following your heart is not following your ordinary desires: it is acknowledging the luminous indwelling intent that naturally extends from your heart and encompasses all being, all manifest aspects of this great vision. It is a reflection of the intent of essence that all may experience this oneness and follow its light safely to fruition. This intent makes itself known not through contemplations of openness and compassion, but the actual experience of opening your heart, entering what you already are, touching it, feeling it with a passion outside of thought, a love beyond desire, and a surrender without loss.

The intent of the essence within this entire unfolding vision is that all beings return to origin, acknowledge their own true nature, and follow the path back home. Openness as a natural knowing is an aspect of this larger intent. It arises as a feeling, a force within your heart, not as a cognitive expression of a purpose, but more like a wordless prayer, a concentric ring expanding outward. This reflection of the larger intent will propel you forward along the path to origin. It is an actual energy, like the life in a seed bursting forth and pushing up from the root through the soil to reach the light. This personal intent is not separate from the intent woven throughout the fabric of being. It has the strength and resolve of a mountain and the fluidity and expansiveness of the ocean, and it moves you toward resolution, the truth that you already are, felt and experienced within your heart.

The intent within your heart is fluid, expansive, and unbounded. Its basis is oneness, and to meet this intent is to touch the initiating force behind it. An open heart connects you; you blend, you touch union, a purpose at the very core of all manifestation, so that the essence may reflect back to itself in you and all beings. Anyone who truly opens his or her heart touches this expansive prayer, limitless, universal, a love outside of time.

The Choice

The intent of the essence within this manifest world includes the ability to choose. We are here to learn spiritually, and there is a spiritual choice that everyone must make, a choice all the more crucial now with the accelerating scope of the intellect. It is a choice of aligning your deepest resolve, your personal will, with your heart or aligning it with your mind. This is a pivotal choice: it determines the outcome of the path. The path of the heart brings you to the oneness of true resolution, a timeless merging beyond union and separation. The path of the mind will not bring you to the full resolution of radiance, will not bring you to your heart blended with the heart of the essence. Instead, it can take you to the realms of power, elaboration, formalism, and holding to doctrine.

You need to know why you are doing spiritual practice in the first place. Ask your heart, be very honest with yourself. How much are you using spiritual practice to fortify rather than dismantle personal identity and a sense of special self? How much are you using your practice to create a spiritual ego? To cultivate a practice that reinforces opaque mind or inflates self-identity clothed as spiritual insight and prowess will blind you and distort your perceptions. The intellect can make you think you are having spiritual experiences, and it can commandeer heart energies and shape them to its own purposes, creating simulated emotions based on comparisons and judgments that distort true heart values of love, compassion, and thankfulness. The heart is the natural seat of your being, and when you break through the entanglements of the intellect and reclaim the translucent inward power of your heart, you will naturally come to deeper experiences of openness, with more willingness to relate, and more love, compassion, and gratitude welling up spontaneously from your heart that will propel you along the path to a timeless merging with origin.

Perseverance and Surrender

The art of spiritual practice is one of remaining within openness in a way that does not solidify a new sense of self-identity around perseverance on the path. Staying with openness in a blended responsive way, remaining connected rather than distanced from whatever passes into the field of that openness, is natural for the heart. For separate identity upheld by the mind, perseverance means to hold to a fixed position, a stance, a view, and surrender is failure and loss. Yet from the heart's perspective, perseverance and surrender are one fluid whole, a movement of embrace, opening freely, blending without fear, not using ideas of emptiness or positive thinking to dismiss the impact of whatever you meet, but meeting whole-heartedly just as it is, your openness enfolding and embracing rather than pulling back. The ability to remain open within the widening view of full engagement comes from the heart. For the heart there is no separation between perseverance and surrender, they are one essential act.

Surrendering to Your Heart

Shifting your energy from being centered in the intellect to being centered in the heart is pivotal to entering the inclusive expansive openness that is our natural way of being. The following meditation can be helpful in guiding the mind toward letting go of control and allowing the heart to come forward as the basis of your experience.

The first step is to bring yourself to a calm state, like water in a still pond. It is best to begin by lying down in a warm comfortable place. Later as you become more accustomed to this practice, you can go into the meditation in any posture, but at first, lie down on your back with your hands at your sides and your legs uncrossed. Take a few moments to settle in, then take a deep breath and hold it, tense all the muscles of your body all at once and then release them completely as you breathe out. You may want to tense different parts of your body sequentially, beginning at your feet, with a series of breaths. Eventually you will only need a single deep breath with a slight pause and a faint muscle tension to release and relax. Imagine that you are standing in a shower of vibrant white light. Feel the light pouring all around you and into the crown of your head and down through your body to your feet. This light begins to fill your body from your feet upward like bright living water filling a clear glass.

Once your whole body is glowing, rest in that for a few gentle breaths. Take another deep breath, hold it briefly, and then let it all out, surrendering to your heart. This is a feeling outside of words, outside of knowing how; you give yourself completely to the energy of your heart. Feel the relaxed weight of your body sinking slowly toward the Earth. Then out of that sinking, melting feeling, you begin to float upward as the brightness that you are lifts up out of the weight. You can rest and refresh yourself in the floating brightness for a while, or you can continue into another meditation.

Body of Light

A simple yet profound way to recognize and accept the radiant openness already within you is to move with it. First, center yourself and surrender to your heart while standing, keeping your eyes open in wide-angle vision. Imagine your body made of rainbow light, translucent and shimmering, one step in front of you, facing in the same direction that you are facing. Any physical ailments that you may have are not there. Any self-limiting ideas or feelings of inadequacies are also absent. Then slowly step into the body of light, as if you were water pouring into a clear glass. Feel yourself becoming the perfection, shimmering with light and seeing through eyes of light.

Remain standing and allow your body of light to slowly sit down where you are, turning a quarter circle to the right or left in a slow spiral as it descends, seeing clearly through its eyes, seeing the landscape change as your vantage point lowers and rotates. Once the body of light is sitting, continue looking around at the landscape through its eyes for a few moments. Then as you remain focused in the view from the light body, slowly allow your physical body to sit down into it, turning as you descend. Once your physical body is settled sitting within the body of light, the body of light slowly stands up turning another quarter circle in the same direction as before, while the physical body remains sitting. Again, pay attention to the view through your eyes of light as it rises and turns. Once your body of light is standing, look around through its eyes, and then slowly allow your physical body to stand up into the body of light repeating the same spiraling movement. Continue sitting and standing a number of times, then sit and remain in that acknowledged space. This can be a very effective way to shift your perceptions and recognize that you are not confined within your physical body or your ordinary states of mind and habits of identity. It is particularly effective when done outdoors. You can see details of the landscape through the eyes of your light body that you may not have seen through your regular eyes, and you may come to realize a blended sense of being with the natural world you had not encountered before.

Dreaming

The mind tends to compartmentalize and keep outer and inner experience separate, but experiences of the heart are interactive and inclusive. We share a natural flow of experience with all beings. As you recognize this permeable quality, subjective and objective lose their defining boundaries. You begin to erase the border between perception and participation in a dynamic communicative world. Dreams, signs, and visions become meaningful aspects of your life as you open your heart and respond, recognizing that you are already immersed in a vast ocean of experience in which nothing is separate and everything is alive.

Dreaming can provide another way to access perceptions outside the familiar limits of the physical senses. Personal and transcendent, shadow and light, past, present, and future, possible and impossible, all worlds intertwined, learning to orient yourself within this fluid sphere can help you greatly along the path. Dreaming offers an arena in which you can shift the habits of mind and its insistence on solidity, time, and space and can help you recognize the visionary quality of all your experience. There are many methods to engage this energy and numerous books have been written about techniques for dreaming. The basic choice is to intervene in the process or allow it to happen. You can cultivate becoming aware within a dream while you are dreaming by locating an object or scene that you have chosen and focused on before you go to sleep, but you run the risk of limiting the natural expansiveness of the dreaming state by the choices and concerns of the mind.

You can choose instead to be more open and attentive to whatever the dreaming presents to you, respecting the dreams as clues to a more fluid knowing outside your normal waking mind. Very much like waiting for animals without expectation or manipulation, you open to another dimension of experience, a deeper level of dreaming through which the wholeness of your heart can also speak to you and share with you its ability to communicate spontaneously in a flowing natural way. Finding a way in waking life to acknowledge your dreaming life, by making gestures related to the content of a dream, or drawing simple pictures or diagrams from the dreams, anything to let the dreaming know that you are paying attention, will deepen your relationship with the processes already ripening within you.

Signs

As you open to your heart, you become more aware of your heart's connection with the heart of all life. You begin to recognize the specific ways that the essence is communicating with you in waking life. Signs and omens arise as messages, radiant expressions of the essence. But understanding and knowing how to interpret these signs involves a true listening in your heart, and it takes time to learn how to see, hear, feel, and touch these messages without embellishing or projecting. This comes from practice, from settling into our mother the Earth, and surrendering to your heart.

Synchronicities, natural phenomena, and the behavior of animals and insects may give warnings or clues, directions and answers to choices you need to make, or indicate future events long before they happen. All manner of communications are possible within the living interrelationships of the shared vision of life we call this world. They may arise to startle you, shake you, or gently guide you, through events that are clearly outside the patterns of ordinary habitual life. Animals may act in ways that are uncharacteristic for them, with unusual behavior, or familiar behavior that is unusually close to you or relating directly with you in some way, as when a bird calls as it flies low over your head or a fox walks right up to you. When you begin to experience this deeper communication, be sensitive to the varying factors all around you at the moment of the sign: the time of day, position of the sun or moon, cardinal directions, and any other relational aspect that comes to the attention of your heart. Allow all of these aspects to paint a picture that you feel intuitively. Do not force it, but let the picture settle into your heart; awareness and a knowing will arise within you.

Vision Quest

The vision quest has been taught within many traditional cultures. It is an ancient way to open to your heart and experience a deeper communication with the essence that can guide you through the rest of your life. There are numerous ways to approach this sacred practice of time apart in the wilderness, which usually involves fasting from all food and in some traditions from water as well, and various preparations, ceremonies, and number of days spent on a quest. Rather than offer guidelines here, we would like to share some aspects of questing we have experienced that are relevant to blending your heart with the heart of the essence.

When you take the first step into your quest circle, you have already prayed for guidance and given thanks to all life, all teachers. As you cross the threshold into a vision quest, you leave everything outside your circle, all prayers, all spiritual practice, and all the concerns and worries of your life. You enter into a sphere of simplicity, a time of openness, an embrace within the radiance of origin, and your only duty is to be open and aware, to see and hear with your heart the teachings that will be imparted to you about your life's path. You pay respectful attention to everything going on around you. The intent of essence is speaking to you through the natural world, through the animals, birds, and insects, plants and trees, the sun and moon, and also through the visionary pathway of your heart. It is truly a time held within the heart and basis of all experience. There is only openness and your ability to wait, waiting without filling up the space with anything else, waiting without waiting, settling within an undefined and open space. This experience leads you to an even deeper opening of your heart, for there is a fluid potency within this waiting, feeling the rhythms of the essence, which opens a visionary doorway.

There are many concepts about visionary experience, but the point is to come to your vision quest purely from your heart, with an openness to whatever may arise. Watch and feel everything that is presented to you, from a sunset to the tiniest insect or a soft breeze. Open with gratitude to all that speaks to you in the countless voices of the essence, focusing, like the sun's rays through a single drop of water, all your intent and heart into a single circle of experience that opens beyond time.

Hell Sit

In a vision quest, you are opening to the radiance of the essence, entering into resonance with this primordial intent, trusting and blending with a generosity far outside the scope of self. In a hell sit, you learn to trust the openness of your heart in the face of negative forces that are decidedly not generous, that are hostile and holding to separation. A hell sit is an experience of maintaining openness and love for all life in the face of fear. It breaks down barriers within yourself that have held you back and strengthens your commitment to complete the path and bring benefit to all life.

This kind of experience not only brings you up against your own negativity, but also puts you in contact with negative forces that condense within the fabric of this world. Certain places hold the energies of harmful actions and emotions very strongly, drawn to and intensified by negative forces far older than human activity. Often spirits are also attracted to these energies and can cling there. They can be seen as dull lights or shadows and are as varied as all the degrees of emotion and energy that they are drawn to.

The single most important aspect of this practice is to know your purpose, the intent of your spiritual life. As you embark on the spiritual path, at first you may be focused on increasing positive qualities and circumstances for yourself and others. As your connection to the intent within your heart strengthens, you trust that connection, and your practice becomes a living prayer integrated with the radiant intent of the essence, a prayer for all life, a prayer that all beings, positive or negative without judgment, acknowledge and return to the blended state of oneness. This is a deep-seated love, a reflection of the very compassion that fostered you. It is this core love that can hold at bay all the demons throughout space. This intent is not a power to overcome or subdue, but a compassionate force, a cellular love, which enters the hearts of all beings, an intent beyond self, encompassing all.

Sitting with negative energies is best undertaken in the care of an experienced guide who can place you on an appropriate spot for your spiritual growth. Then, alone, usually at night in an isolated place or woodland, in an environment that is negative but not outwardly dangerous, you abide with your purpose, confronting not only the negative forces around you but also the uncontrolled nature of your mind. This experience forces you to see how your mind on its own adds to the outward development of any experience. If your mind stands down and aligns itself with the natural openness of your heart, an expansive love with an intention to benefit all beings within this shared vision of life, then the negative entities that come will pass you by. They may put you to the test, pushing you to your limits, but they will subside, their power weakened by the love pouring over them. But if your thoughts run away with fear, anger, or other negative emotions and feelings, the entities will grow in strength. They will harass you, overtake your mind, or even bring about your death. Through the hell sit, you can come to a genuine confidence in the power of spiritual practice as you experience directly the depth of the intent within your heart and the fading of negative forces. You also come to a more expansive view of the negative forces themselves, seeing them as teachers. The truth of this life is that the radiance of the essence pushes and pulls us in myriad ways to guide and teach.

The Charnel Ground

The charnel ground encompasses a much larger dynamic than a hell sit in a fearful place. The cremation grounds of ancient India were set apart on the outskirts of cities and were revered by spiritual practitioners of many different paths. Amid rotting corpses, scattered bones, roving spirits, and the stench of decay, practitioners also found wildflowers, songbirds, open sky, and forests of fragrant trees. They found a natural freedom in these places, uncultivated, unrestrained, and intense, with danger, death, and a wild beauty both delicate and raw, seldom frequented except by those seeking to go outside the domination of the mind and reach the heart. The charnel ground is the borderland between true wilderness and the structures of culture, the meeting ground of the known, the unknown, and the unknowable. It is a place of letting go, the place of death, the corpse, the forces of decay, a gap that allows the dissolution of your opaque, acculturated mind, a place of transition and transformation, a place of dissolution and resolution.

The charnel ground is another aspect of the sacred intent in your heart. This intent takes you out of your ordinary concepts and perceptions and forces you, confronts you, demands that you see everything as it is, the good and the bad. You are compelled to go to places that will move you, challenge you, and shift your perceptions utterly, and coupled with a deep desire and love to benefit all life, this will propel you forcefully along your path. Like true renunciation, the charnel ground is not so much cultivated as it is honored when it arises, but like waiting for animals, you can watch and be ready for it, and accept its presence in your life with a thankful heart.

As your willingness to let go beyond yourself gains strength and momentum and your intent enlarges in scope, you may find yourself changing significant aspects of your life. This may be a natural outgrowth of your progress in changing habits of identity or perception, or it may be a parallel process already in motion ripening at its own pace and in its own way, as it did for us. The pattern of renunciation developing over many lives may be awakening on its own. Careers, family, friends, home, land, financial security, jobs, achievements, major categories of hard-won identity, you may find yourself shedding them unexpectedly. Fragile, brittle, tissue-thin, they slough off easily, you cannot hold them if you try. You find yourself strangely vulnerable and free at the same time, open in what will perhaps seem to others a precarious and perilous way. You have accomplished an important and difficult aspect of the path; you have reached the charnel ground within yourself.

The charnel ground can arise in many ways, in any life, in any culture or time. We found our charnel ground in outer landscapes both urban and wilderness, and in the choices we made to totally alter our way of life: moving to new areas, changing the way we lived and worked, and how we defined ourselves. The charnel ground is an organic expression of your spiritual life as you begin to see through the overlay of ordinary identities, a movement within your whole being, a force driving you to leave your familiar world and enter the wilderness, the unknown. If you are compelled from your deepest heart to enter the charnel ground, you enter a freedom to see and learn beyond ordinary constructs. You realize a crucial, vital space within you, an opening for new energy to move upward and unmask the essence that you already are.

The Spiritual Path

In earlier times, before the fall from original heart and Earth, when a man or a woman felt within their hearts a clear call, a burning desire and need to let go into a process of transformation already at work deep within them, these original people left all that they knew and loved to find a blended experience of oneness with the natural radiance of essence in the wilderness. They began to wander with a calling in their hearts, searching for a spiritual guide, having reached an important stage on the path, an important decision. They may have known how to find water, shelter, and food, but this journey could take months or years, and these ancient followers of the heart had to have great courage to take the first step. In this experience, they already had an open heart and knew how to follow this timeless call. They knew how to listen and find the call within their direct experience.

The Role of the Guide

The role of the guide is to be a doorway to your own direct experience of the radiant intent of the essence. The ultimate guide is the essence. The radiance of origin as nature is the guidance, always there if you are truly open, the basis of spiritual life and visionary experience. An animal, a plant, mountains, rivers, the soil under your feet can teach beyond words the lessons of the universe. They are the voice of the essence, a natural call for reunion sounding within your heart, personal and direct, spiritual life as vision.

A human guide can show you aspects that you may have missed and push, pull, prod, or lead you in directions you may not have seen, but a true guide also knows that he or she is only a pointer for the next generation to experience the patterns of fruition already woven within this arising vision of life. A guide is also humble in the act of initiating a change in the student. Guides know they are only helping others toward their own direct experience of the intent of the essence. They are one within the vision that is this life, and once they have offered their vision to the next generation, they will pass from this life. They care nothing for titles, lineage, or other external authorization. They are a simple, humble part of this manifest realm. Being in direct contact with such a person can initiate a profound change in your very being. It is like opening yourself up to a river, coming to know the river's life cycle, coming to hear in your heart the teachings of the rhythm and flow of the river's heart changing you like water smoothes a stone. In the same way, a true guide affects your heart with their very being.

A human guide has accomplished the whole path, the reunion with essence, the resolution of radiance. For them, nothing less is acceptable. He or she is now here for all life, not just human. He or she is a constant ripple of concentric rings, fluid and soft, stretching out upon a pond's surface. Most people would not notice a true guide; most are seeking attributes associated with concepts of authority. The true guide is unencumbered by these concepts and will be like a weathered stone along a path, easily missed by those whose eyes are dazzled by hopes of power, fame, and grandeur. The true guide is here for those who have an open heart and the courage and perseverance to overcome the limiting ideas and perceptions that maintain the personal container of self. Their guidance is simple yet profound, a gesture toward direct experience of those whom he or she is guiding. The important part of guiding is to help them reach fruition, to see the vision that is this life through the eyes of the vision itself, the eyes of inner radiance. The guide is a natural part of this manifest world and those who seek a guide are just as humble. They have no other desire but a movement in their heart, a courage to experience the essence as the essence, as a dewdrop falls upon the surface of a pond.

The true guides in nature, vision, or in human form are the radiance of origin naturally so, unencumbered by culture or doctrine. They are one with all that naturally arises. The stone weathering along the path is blended with all life; he or she is within all experience, happy or sad, open to the feelings within the currents of their times yet still the stone that weathers, beingness embedded as vision in vision. The goal is not happiness, power, or joy; it is beingness as the heart of all life.

Willingness to Change

Unlike spiritual seekers in early times who could leave their familiar world, followers of the heart in our contemporary world have fewer options to leave society and go into the wilderness to follow a spiritual path. Our world culture has become increasingly complex, and it has become harder to release yourself from the internalized aspects of the mental complexity in which we live. Yet original heart is natural and unelaborate and requires simple means to experience it. The challenge now is all the greater because the worldview dominated by the mind is so omnipresent, and it is difficult to touch the unelaborate truth while still enmeshed in its patterns. To break through these patterns requires a courage that comes from aligning your deepest intent with your heart, with your love.

Most people experience their lives through the expectations and conditions given to them by others, which are then upheld by their minds. Fear of stepping outside convention, outside the safety zone, presents a big problem on the spiritual path. Spiritual practice can unfortunately tap the desire for safety and demand a secure orthodox universe where nothing can disturb the assumed order. Many children, particularly in early childhood, are naturally open to spiritual experience unencumbered by ideas of doctrine. Adults around them often steer them toward the safety zone, away from direct experience of spiritual dimensions that are beyond the established norms, and the experiences can be forgotten or set aside. But the quality of open heart that is so present in early childhood can be embraced again.

The most precious aspect of human birth is that we can choose to change and touch that openness. Being open to change is the basis of creativity and spiritual growth. They are both about opening to the possibilities within this arising vision of life and being willing to try, explore, and even fail. The creative process naturally allows opposites to coexist without holding to either side and can embrace the energy moving between them, allowing a dynamic wholeness to emerge, moving in harmony with the fluidity of all creation. Spiritual practice is an art, not in the sense of making drawings, or paintings, or music, but in the sense of being able to move within and be open to experience outside your boundaries, to be open to grace, to allow yourself into the flow of the ineffable.

The spiritual path will change you. If you have an idea that you can do spiritual practice and keep your ordinary life intact, you are mistaken and your mind has control over your heart. You will change. Your life will not be one of structure, of holding to preconceived concepts of normal life. You enter a river that flows to the sea, fluid and expansive, not linear, a path of heart toward a blended embrace.

Fear

The biggest obstacle to being willing to change is fear. As you move along the spiritual path you naturally encounter fear in many forms, not only fears associated with danger or death, but also fears associated with the spiritual path itself: fear of confronting the shadow side of your mind, your experiences and memories and currents of habits from past lives; fear of letting go of your familiar, smaller self; fear of the naturally fluid, ephemeral nature of experience, the lack of inherent solidity of the structures of this or any life, fear that there is nothing there; fear of the world of spirits, fear of the entities that are moving around us all the time; or fear of the true radiance and joy of light, a brilliance that can be overwhelming in its splendor.

Whatever fear arises, in whatever situation it comes up for you, the only way to deal with it is to just keep going, keep practicing. You do not deny your fear; you still act appropriately in relation to the dangers of this world. You have an intent to follow a spiritual life, and you do your best to stay alive to see it through. You do not run from your fear or let it stop you from learning on the path, but you can be skillful in how you engage with it. If you find that you are sitting on a bad spot and it is bringing up a heavy fear that honestly seems beyond your ability to deal with at that time, you may want to move to another area with the intention to set up good circumstances to strengthen your resolve to deal with it in the future.

Being honest with yourself is crucial. Some people have already given in to fear but they are not aware that they have conceded to it. They may not feel afraid, but they stop learning, and they back away from spiritual growth, from the challenges of letting go. Someone who has lost to fear has closed his or her heart and has been enslaved by their mind. They may be either timid or intimidating in their behavior, but people who have lost to fear want to keep their attachments; they do not want to let go anymore. The gift of life is here for us to do the best we can to learn and grow. You have to take a chance, you may even get hurt along the way, but the courage to move beyond fear is already within your heart and the heart of every being, waiting to be accessed, courage meeting courage, a definitive choice, the courage to be unafraid. Fears belong to the smaller holding self. Courage belongs to a wider scope of the heart's intent, to a commitment to blending beyond self, into a wider embrace. The choice is yours.

Meditative Experience

Once you have embarked on a spiritual path, and are willing to open to deepening levels of experience, you will encounter a number of meditative states that may arise on any spiritual path. Bliss, clarity, and non-thought arise naturally in varying degrees, and it is important to be aware of them so you do not become caught up in them and are able to move with them and through them without holding. None of these experiences are wrong or harmful; they are actually signs of progress. But as they arise, they may seem so fresh and wonderful, so different from how your practice has been before, that you can become very attached to these meditative states. The key to the path is to let go and not hold to anything, let your heart be open, allowing whatever arises to come and go. Bliss, clarity, and non-thought can arise throughout your spiritual life, so you need to learn to ride these experiences without grasping onto them.

Bliss is one of the most compelling meditative experiences, and it can be difficult to let go of this energetic level of spiritual growth. Bliss is part of the rise of energy moving up the central channel to the crown chakra, and it brings a feeling of great joy, an ecstatic state that can be almost orgasmic. This feeling can help open and energize you during long meditative retreats. The problem comes when practitioners seek and hold to bliss, and make it the focus of their practice. You need to allow bliss to arise and fade without clinging, recognizing that it is a sign of the natural vitality of spiritual experience flowing like an endless stream.

Clarity is a kind of confidence that you touch as your practice becomes less confused, a sense of a clear knowing, a feeling about the path, your practice, and your life that was not there before. The experience of clarity can be dramatic in comparison to your previous meditative states, but you need to realize that it is only a sign, a way to know that you are on the right path. If you hold to it at this stage, you will think you are becoming stable, halting your spiritual growth. True stability is much deeper and does not involve holding, instead it is a quality of being, blended in equilibrium with a fluid wholeness outside of self. So just keep going, no matter how clear and lucid your experience becomes.

Non-thought also arises naturally throughout your spiritual life in varying degrees, from an initial occasional fading of your thoughts to the dissolving of concepts farther along the path. In some traditions non-thought is a goal, but there is a more fundamental awareness underlying non-thought, a blended openness, clear and aware. Again, it is important to not be attached to these states or make one experience better than another. The experience of non-thought is a sign of progress, a quality of the expressed essence moving through you, but you do not hold to it.

All these signs of progress are ephemeral experiences arising within the larger flow of your path. You do not want to let your mind grab or hold to them in any way or create a spiritual identity around them. You want to let go into the movement of your heart opening further carrying you toward the full embrace, the resolution, the blended union with the heart of all.

Certainty

After you have been practicing for some time and know how to let go, you will come to experience a deeper kind of clarity, a sense of accomplishment and understanding, the finger in the light socket, "aha! I've got it" stage. You think that you have really gotten somewhere. You feel a seductive confidence. This is just another stage. It may seem wonderful, but you have to let it go. If you succumb to certainty, you will become overconfident. You will think you know, you will have acquired a new knower. It will blind you, and you will make the mistake of assuming that you have already accomplished the path before you have gone very far, and you can become reckless and squander your spiritual energy.

At every stage of the spiritual path, you will encounter degrees of both certainty and uncertainty. Uncertainty is by far the best support, and when you blend with the heart of the Earth, you will be living as original peoples did moving day by day within a fluid grace of uncertainty. The core of the practice and all experiences of original heart are outside definition, outside the borders that maintain certainties, and so you want to cultivate this way of being that is uncertain, flexible, fluid, and humble.

Power

Power can be a natural outgrowth of the spiritual path. It arises for each practitioner in different ways and at different stages of their development. Some people are born with special abilities, some are fascinated with acquiring powers, and others give them little thought for they are more focused on completing the entire path. Power is not synonymous with spiritual realization or accomplishment. Some highly realized practitioners do not exhibit powers. Some people who manifest extraordinary powers have little or no spiritual realization. Flying through the sky, going through walls, knowing all things, can all come from lesser forms of practice. Power is not a defining aspect of resolving all radiance and abiding in genuine being blended within the essence.

Whenever clairvoyance or other forms of powers begin to arise, they can be an expression of your spiritual growth, but they are not realization, do not hold to them. Let them come and go, or you will fall to this challenge of the spiritual path. Powers can be closely related to the mind and its desire for hierarchies and control. Power gives you a sense that you can manipulate others, and even though you may start with good purpose, you can get lost in this kind of mastery. The power can ensnare you, and you want to control more and more. You lose your openness, dominate situations and others, and if you are not vigilant, you can stray into high-minded cruelty. The power is not really yours. It is an expression of the essence, temporarily moving through you. You really need to stay with your heart, acknowledging that you are a part of the essence moving through all life, honoring this connection with true humbleness, knowing that you still have a long way to go on the path.

Concepts of Enlightenment

We would like to speak here about a very special spiritual challenge that each practitioner comes to decisively at some point along their path, the challenge to accept that the experience of full spiritual maturity is naturally abiding within you, that you are allowed to actualize it, and that you can actualize it. The awakened seed of oneness is not reserved for people of another time or another culture, or for super heroes who live in celestial realms far away; it is not outside you. Fruition is natural to all life. Buddhahood, enlightenment, liberation, realization are all grand labels for what is already indwelling in your heart and pervades the fabric of being.

Awakened heart is vast in scope; it has nothing to do with the mind or the attributes that mind projects on it often as inflated versions of itself. All concepts are impediments, and some concepts ensnare us more than others. Even ideas that inspire you at first can hold you back. You need to go beyond the labels and trust your heart. Your heart is already your connection to openness, and is the seat of the courage to follow this path to origin, leading you toward a direct experience of the fabric of being, the indwelling heritage that all beings share.

Coming home to the embrace of essence is a natural organic process woven into every aspect of this naturally arising vision of life. The experience of blending with origin is outside culture and language, beyond self, beyond concepts of solidity, time, and space, beyond concepts of enlightenment. It is outside the ideas that the mind ascribes to it. The challenge is to go beyond the confines of the mind with its locked down concepts and open your heart like an awakening seed into a knowing of a blended acknowledgement. All aspects of oneness are reflected throughout the fabric of being, expressed in the natural world in the fluidity of water, the openness of sky, the patient generosity of Earth. These are but a few of the abundant qualities that lead us to oneness within this manifest world. You can touch them directly and experience them within your own heart now, outside the limited and limiting boundaries of words and concepts.

Nature

Followers of the heart, mystics of any tradition have a deep heart connection with nature. It is a natural outgrowth of spiritual practice that one is drawn into the intent of the essence through the dynamic beauty and joy of nature. The vision that is this life is the radiance of origin, the intent arising as the natural world in all its variety of place and form to guide all beings to the embrace of the essence. But even in the early stages of spiritual growth you can experience this world as a fluid dance of direct experience. Every moment, every movement within the vision that is this life is alive with sign, dream, and vision. We are already blended into and within this shared vision; let go and slowly slip into the flow of nature to recognize the indwelling heart of all experience.

The blending of your heart with nature is a good sign. Mystics and original spirits of the heart of any time know the natural world is the home, the temple, and the shrine. If you find yourself turning away from nature, away from the Earth and turning instead toward structure and doctrine, it is a sign that your mind has control over your heart and your spiritual practice. If you are drawn more and more to the natural world, toward blending with the vision that is this life, you know you are going in the right direction.

The call to go into the wilderness as part of your spiritual growth is ageless and nearly universal. Even people in cultures that already live in close harmony with the natural world seek time apart in wilderness to deepen their connection with the source of all. It is natural to seek solitude apart from human society of any kind to hear the voices of all life woven from the single voice of the source, to find your spiritual home in the wilderness. Nature is a direct expression of the intent of essence outside the constructs of human language and culture, outside the constraints of human perception and mind. The natural world, rocks, trees, plants, water, air, and Earth are all authentic living expressions of the radiance that provide increasingly crucial support along the path as you shed more and more trappings of the mind.

Illumination

The path already laid out in your heart by the intent of essence unfolds at a different pace for each person, and so there have come to be many different ways of mapping the progression of spiritual growth but there are some stages of spiritual transformation that are intrinsic to many paths.

For many, engagement with the path of the heart begins with an initiatory experience of illumination, a personal encounter with radiance. Illumination is extremely compelling. It can come to you in many ways, whether in dream, vision, near death experience, or a shocking event in your life, and it may be of varying degrees of intensity, from an initial glimpse of indwelling brilliance like the glint of light on water, to a full-blown experience of inner radiance. Illumination has a tone similar to clarity and certainty, but clarity and certainty are colored by the mind, while illumination has the flavor of touching and being touched directly in your heart, a relating with and within a living brilliance. It is an opening, a connection, a relationship. The illumination can be glorious and brings with it a sense of meeting and being met by something luminous beyond self, which can lead to a sense of accomplishment and knowing when the mind grabs onto this experience, but this is only a stage. In whatever form it comes into your life, and it may arise a number of times, know that it is a sign, a guidance toward a true embrace. It is important that you do not become caught up in the experience, suspended on the path, blinded by your own headlights.

Many people have had experiences of illumination and have become overwhelmed by them, leaving their path and going out to teach and elucidate on the incredible experience they have had, and in all this, they lose their energy and resolve to continue. They become stuck in the afterglow. They may seem bright, joyful, and confident, but illumination is only a portal that you must enter and then pass through. Illumination is one of the first major acknowledgements of the intent of the essence, a taste, a touch, a sometimes not so gentle brilliant slap in the face. Illumination, though glorious and wonderful, and so compelling that you want everyone to know about it, is fundamentally a personal experience, and when disentangled from the mind's attempts to co-opt and exploit it, becomes a secret memory, a longing in your heart, a yearning to be touched again by its grace in every new experience. It is a reflection of the source and a marker for the direction of return to original heart.

The Night

The night is a spiritual night, a silence of light where the glow from illumination dies to nothing and you are left on the path seemingly in the dark. It is sometimes referred to as the dark night of the soul, but the experience of the night does not need to hold the dread that this phrase can engender. The night brings an inward turning, a quietness that pervades your spiritual path. You may feel that nothing speaks to you and that grace has left you. You are left alone on the path, waiting with an unknowing knowing, a simple trust. Grace has not gone away; it is speaking to you with a different voice, and in the silence of this night, you are learning to listen and surrender from a deeper level of your heart.

The angst quality of this stage of the path only arises if you are not letting go, if you are holding with your mind to an experience of illumination and resisting the changes that are already coming to you. Within the quiet loss of illumination, you learn to listen in the dark silence to something new. Staying with your heart no matter what you are feeling keeps you in touch with grace. This is a powerful time. You are learning to listen beyond words, trust beyond trust, see beyond light. You are shifting your center of gravity to another dimension of experience.

Crossing the Pass

As you continue to progress along the heart's path, eventually after years of concerted practice you will come to the stage at which your acknowledgment of original heart becomes an ongoing experience, no longer separate moments of clear awareness brightening the path and then dying away to be again recalled. Now the glimpse that you had during the illumination stage of an open engaged radiance has been allowed to arise from your heart again and again within the immediacy of your direct experience. Recognized without holding and grasping, it has become part of your life. You have crossed an important threshold. The clouds of one's mind are no longer obscuring the breath of the essence in your heart and pervading all existence. Now original heart is an ongoing state, a natural organic connection with the underlying foundation of the vision that is this life, a living acknowledgement that you are part of the fabric of being. Most people do not get this far; many become stuck within their minds, thinking and simulating the stages of the path. Crossing the pass is a gentle glory and a great happiness that arises from the sky of your heart like the dawn in early spring, touching all life.

The Embrace

Within the embrace, there are no more stages; there is no further path. It is an experience of total and complete resolution of all being, your sphere of influence blended effortlessly into the essence, like water into water, a seamless oneness.

The culmination of the spiritual path has many words and concepts associated with it. Doctrine and even politics have worked their way into belief systems about the final passage, through attempts to define or harness it in human terms. Completion is inherent in the path from the beginning, woven into the fabric of being, woven into the radiance. Following the motion of a circle, the path comes around to meet itself, a time of resolution, the final letting go, the final relinquishing, a time of passage into an awakened life. This is a natural cycle, a movement within all cycles of the universe, and the final path is the same, the culmination of the path of letting go into a relationship with the intent of the essence, moving in the flow of a primordial stream. You allow your heart to guide you within an utter embrace. This is not the domain of the mind, but a true engagement with the intent within and beyond all that naturally arises.

At the time of the embrace during the visionary practice of radiance, original heart has been stable for quite a while, free of the constraints of the mind. The world has come alive, revealed as rainbow light, and the essence becomes apparent as the blue-black depth of all. It is just a moment and a step away from complete union, essence into essence.

All that is left is just a shell that becomes gossamer thin as the essence within begins to blend with the essence beyond manifestation, never separate from total and complete union. This is a visceral experience involving all being, your personal sphere of radiance and all that manifests resolving as a seamless whole. Stability in original heart alone does not bring you to this culmination, the resolution of all your being and the world around you. This resolving of the radiance is reached through the completion of the primordial visionary path of radiance. This path of the light found in your heart does not belong to any one group or tradition. The light is its own passage to resolution, free, unowned by any structure. You lay aside all that manifests, all that has guided you up to this point, now a sphere of influence blended within the essence, nothing not nothing, a potential ringing with intent, a true embrace.

Decline

Whether you have reached the resolution in this life or not, you will face the natural process of decline one way or another. The decline is a movement of turning inward, the completion of the circle. It can be a turning inward of personal self toward childhood memories, or a turning inward of the wider scope of the embrace. If you have given into fear, illumination, or power, you will turn the more constricted scope of those energies inward. You do not escape the inward turning; however far you have gotten along the path when you reach the decline, you turn the summation of that experience inward to set the seed of the next life.

If you have not completed the path before old age envelops you, you run the risk of giving in to tiredness and other basic afflictions of old age that can sap your energy and your resolve to persevere. You can become fixated on eternal life or on other forms of salvation elsewhere in heavenly or pure realms. In linear expansionist cultures, obsessed with forward progress, there is a widespread fear of the cyclical aspects of life and experience, and especially a fear of the natural cycle of decline. The desire for eternal youth and powers to fight off or deny the decline into death comes from not understanding the self-surrender of setting seed, and can be an obstacle at this stage of life.

The last part of the practice, the last part of the path, may well be the hardest even without old age, and you will need all your strength and openness fully engaged here, now.

Depending on the pattern of your life, the decline can come at any time. You begin to see that your life is cresting, turning toward the dissolution. If your life path allows, you will grow into old age, but you can also face a critical illness or sudden death at any age, and in those cases, the decline will be drastically compressed. As your life energies begin to crest, you must look into your heart and see the life around you and your responsibility to it; this time is crucial. You must complete your path as far as it will take you, in whatever time your life allows.

If you reach the time of old age, it does not necessarily mean a time of rest. It can be a time of greater determination rooted in a warm joy in your heart, knowing your responsibility to all life and in every step you take expressing the joy that flows from the heart of intent within all that manifests. Many physical problems can arise in old age but your heart knows that you are needed. You may not move with the ease that you once had but there is still a way for you to act and share your heart with others. This is a time of setting the seed for your next life and for the lives of those around you, by focusing on the most essential life-engendering aspects of your experience. If you are a person of heart then the time of final decline into death is not a sad one; it is just another path, for you are always moving in the flow of intent like a ring of light moving farther and farther out on a pond's surface, always blended in brilliance.

Original Heart
Original Nature

Within this great manifest vision are all the clues we need for the path of return to the essence. Sit quietly in a light rain beside a small pool or at the shallow edge of a river. Watch as drops of rain create rings of movement on the surface of the water, concentric circles expanding outward, overlapping and interacting with other circles, the whole surface reflecting the sky. Allow your gaze to unfold your heart within the great heart of all manifesting for you to witness the openness and fluidity of original heart. Sometimes the rain will also make fragile spheres, bubbles floating on the surface, some touching other bubbles, some alone, all seemingly stable until they pop. In the same way, all life is woven of interacting spheres of being emanating from and then returning to the essence.

Inner experience of the all-pervasive essence is found within our personal sphere of being. The acknowledgement of this involves a subtle shift. You see the contrast between the confined yet ephemeral aspects of mind and the true sky of your heart, an embrace of all being, an openness natural and abiding. Within this expansive sky-like experience, there is a sense of knowing, a knowing outside any conceptualization, an openness that has no boundaries, edges, or restrictions of any kind. This is original heart, none other than the recognized nature of the essence reflecting out of your heart and all creation. Our eyes, the globe of the Earth, a dew drop on the tip of a leaf, the ultimate, profound, amazing truth is everywhere all around us and within us right now, indwelling yet all-pervasive, personal yet unlimited.

If you follow and live with our suggestions in previous chapters for entering into direct experience of the heart within the natural world, if you really give yourself time to be open to whatever arises, you will come naturally to these sky-like moments of original heart as part of the flow of your experience. This chapter is about deepening and remaining in this primordial experience of openness.

Original heart is a natural expression of the essence already abiding in our hearts, our birthright that has been covered over and occluded by formal systems of religious and spiritual practice that arose as people turned away from the Earth. The blended acknowledgement of the openness abiding within, would have been naturally part of the spiritual experience of original peoples of the Earth, arising directly out of their daily life with the wilderness. This primordial gift is still within each of us, and we can enter directly into the flow of original heart through the radiance that is here all around us, arising as the shared vision we call life.

The Four Acknowledgements

There are four guiding acknowledgements of the path of primordial grace: openness, transcendence, spontaneous presence, and oneness. They are each facets of primordial grace and are traditionally introduced to guide you to deepening experience of the blended openness of original heart that is indwelling in your heart and in the natural world. The complete path involves the union of original heart and the visions of radiance, and the four acknowledgements are its general framework of grace imbedded into the fabric of being. Openness and transcendence are more closely related to the practice of original heart, while spontaneous presence and oneness are associated with the visionary experience of radiance.

You may have already touched one or more of the acknowledgments through some of the practices we have suggested earlier, or they may have arisen naturally for you in the course of your life. Like the four qualities of the Earth, they are aspects of a seamless whole that you experience decisively as you reach fruition in the visionary practice of radiance, but you can begin to access all four qualities within the natural radiance of this world. They are reflections of the intent of the essence intrinsic to our experience of this world, and they are within you right now. People originally lived within the flow of these aspects without needing to differentiate them before the split between mind and heart. Now they are an aid to help your mind acknowledge and appreciate the truly vast scope of your heart's perceptions and the depth of aware experience available to you. But emphasis on clearing the perceptions of the mind is not enough. After recognizing the four qualities, you need to begin interacting with the radiance manifesting as this world directly in your own experience within original heart. You need to look through its eyes.

Openness

If you live from your heart with the Earth, you will naturally come to experience the quality of openness as it is expressed directly by the radiance of the essence. Openness is right here all around you. It helps you experience what is becoming evident within your heart. Openness is seen in the vast blue sky. Openness is the sky. When you can recognize this quality in a heartfelt, intuitive way, you become aware that it remains, it abides. Watch the sky, it will guide you, it will teach you this expression of the essence. The sky, blue, expansive, and vast, can have clouds forming, moist and billowing, or heavy fog, enveloping and dense, or rain, or snow, but the sky remains, and you know this in your heart. Emotions or habits of mind will arise and yet you know the sky of your heart remains, it abides, and in this acknowledgement the emotions or whatever will fade, will seem less real, less significant. By recognizing and remaining, abiding and allowing, the clouds begin to part and slowly fade away.

Transcendence

As you recognize the sky-like quality of openness, you also feel a tone within your heart that has no true name or character to pinpoint. This sense or feeling, ineffable, aware, is the depth of your heart and the depth of everything, beyond the you looking at the sky, beyond sky, undefined, with a knowing outside of concept, a depth of experience. It is like descending into a cave far, far below the surface of the Earth, and in a vast cavern you turn off the lights and rest within absolute darkness, absolute depth. You are standing within the depth of your heart, knowing without knowing; in the same way, transcendence is a tone of the radiance of origin beyond explanation or description.

Spontaneous Presence

All manifest form is an expression of spontaneous presence, the energy of how things arise. You only need to wait for the dawn on a clear dark night, witnessing the world coming alive in light and color moment by moment, to experience a taste of spontaneous presence, the ephemeral yet ceaselessly arising nature of all phenomena. In the practice of the visions of radiance, you meet this expressive power of the essence directly. No longer shaped through the lens of ordinary perceptions, the pure primordial delight of creation appears as shimmering transparent fluid colors, lines, and forms, and you begin to experience the radiance of the essence free of the limiting avenues of time and space, free of concepts and mind. Within the totally open and transcendent quality of your acknowledged original heart you enter the visionary path of radiance, and the essence seed in your heart begins to sprout and grow, initiating the primordial spontaneously arising cycle of return to origin through the ripening and resolution of radiance.

The natural world arises in the same way as the visions of radiance, as a guidance for the return to essence, and a fundamental aspect of spiritual practice is to blend with this spontaneously arising intent all around us in nature. This quality of spontaneous presence is why we call nature the vision that is this life. The natural world unfolds in a fluid wash moment by moment and comes alive for you if your heart is open and you blend with its movement, its flow. Watch the sky, the waters, the forests, feel their arising force within you and you will know spontaneous presence within your own life.

When you come to acknowledge original heart knowing spontaneous presence as a friend, an integral aspect of the vision that is this life, then there is no cutting through, as recognition of original heart is sometimes called. Cutting through is a process of a solidifying mind that does not allow the fluid spontaneous arising nature of the heart to open and does not acknowledge the equally fluid spontaneous expression of the intent of essence within the natural world. This mind is trying to find original heart within the limits of its own domain, and so it is confined to an experience based solely on cutting from one set of words and concepts to another, ritual games that only allude to freedom. When you acknowledge original heart within the true wholeness of the path instead, then practice is a joy and a fulfillment, a blending with essence already abiding in your heart and in all that naturally arises, moment by moment, spontaneously.

Transcendence and openness are doorways, key acknowledgements to allow the mind to accept dimensions of experience outside its more limited areas of expertise. Openness allows the mind to accept, respect, and listen to the energies of the heart.

Transcendence helps the mind let go of holding to fixed patterns, to requiring all experience to be reducible to something it can handle on its own terms. But neither openness nor the ineffability of transcendence are sufficient introduction to the wholeness of the path. The mind, no matter how free it perceives its view to be, is still working within its own codes, its own limitations. The ability of the heart to embrace experience in a much more dynamic, fluid, feeling way gives true access to the wholeness at the core of all experience. That is why we have emphasized the heart in all our writings and teachings. Not everyone will follow the visionary path of radiance in this life, but everyone is born with the capacity to live from original heart, to touch and be touched by the radiance of the essence shining throughout all that naturally arises.

To seek original heart by training only through recognitions of the mind is futile. You have no basis on which to start, no real connection with your heart. Original heart is not a higher consciousness of mind to which you ascend. Original heart is direct perception of and by the heart of the aware fluid arising nature of the essence woven throughout all of creation. It is simply an acknowledgement from your heart of the heart of all. It is snowfall at twilight, a summer breeze, the wings of a butterfly, a rainbow in a misty sky. It is your wonder at the almost inexpressible beauty and tenderness woven throughout all being.

Oneness

In the visionary path of radiance, the four qualities come together as one through the resolution of the path. The visions of primordial light bring you to union, wholeness, and the release of all separation through direct experience of the spontaneously arising nature of anything and everything as a single seamless radiant expression of the essence.

There are many levels or degrees of the experience of oneness, from the oneness as you open your heart to encompass the hopes and fears of all beings, to the oneness of pure essence. You may have already touched an aspect of oneness while waiting for animals, witnessing the interrelated concentric rings of being, and later as your practice deepened, you may have felt that all myriad manifestation also moves within your heart. There is an even deeper and inconceivably comprehensive level of oneness that you come to through the visions of radiance. The visions connect you directly to the essence seed in your heart in a way at once personal yet not separate from the essence and all that arises from its radiance. As you approach resolution in these visions of light, oneness dawns beyond time or space, within a purity of light at the very edge of the essence until the moment when all phenomena resolve and only essence remains, a knowing beyond knowing, absolute potential, absolute intent, the seamless single depth of oneness.

Oneness is woven throughout the vision that is this life, and when you enter the natural world with an open heart, you will come to experience a blended bonded feeling that is inexpressible. This is not the same as the culminating oneness of resolution in the visions of radiance, but it is a touch, a taste, a glimpse expressed within the sphere of this life, like the barest brilliance of morning light through the trees. As you continue to live and blend with nature, you will feel in your heart an all-encompassing tone of connection, feeling it seamlessly within your heart. All aspects of the cycle of spiritual growth are found at all levels; you will not have a complete experience of oneness until the resolution of radiance, though you need to experience this quality of blended acknowledgement of the heart in some way all along the path. It is a guiding force, the intent of the essence speaking to you through the visionary experience that is life.

Oneness is the heart of the spiritual path, the circle through which you are moving home, and at the same time, home itself at every step along the way. You are never apart from the natural intrinsic wholeness of the fabric of being. You have never been apart from the essence, you are already home, there have never been any divisions. The path of return to origin is the path of deeply experiencing this underlying oneness that is already around you and within you right now, but you come to degrees of this experience gradually. One very accessible expression of the all-inclusive oneness already in your life is the web of living energies sometimes imaged as Indra's net.

This luminous web of intent, a reflection of the living continuum of the radiance of essence, which arises vividly as the lattices of light in the visions of radiance, can be experienced directly within the vision that is this life through opening your heart to another in genuine compassion and love. The jewels at the crossroads of the net can be holy beings, friends, mountains, plants, waters, rivers, oceans, a dewdrop, the light on a windowsill. The essential aspect is the luminous heart to heart connection with all life, the acknowledgement of the primordial essence in all. We are already an integral part of this sacred net of great compassion. Our choice is to open to it and bond with this great union. This ability to bond heart to heart within your life is a measure of your ability to bond with the visions, and without this capacity and willingness to relate, the visions will not unfold in an authentic way.

Feeling oneness in your heart is essential for your practice, and as your experience of oneness deepens, original heart can open gently, delicately more and more until it blossoms as the fullness of inner radiance, and you take the last path in which all patterns of energy and manifestation become experienced as truly whole.

Original Heart

Original heart is the natural state of the human heart, fluid, aware, blended with the intent of essence. It arises; it is not constructed or visualized, not conjured out of thoughts or words. It is not a concept to ascribe to, nor is it a doctrine to be understood and then followed. The true experience of original heart can arise clearly and purely when you touch and are touched by the natural world, a living breathing active blessing speaking to your heart, touching your heart with the rainbow brilliance of sunrise through a dewdrop or an ice crystal, a bright hello popping you out of your shell. Original heart is a glow or brilliance in the heart of all life, simple and natural, in which we all can and should abide, in full acknowledgement of its abiding nature already within us.

You need not go far to encounter it. Everyone has experienced it at some point in their lives. You are born with an open aware heart. Unfortunately, most humans have allowed their minds to dominate their hearts. We are taught from earliest childhood by initiates of our agreed reality to perceive and function in a world mediated almost entirely by the mind, and in that context, genuine experience of original heart can seem rare and illusive when in fact it is our natural home.

Many people who come to spiritual practice today fall to the prevailing problem of thinking their feelings and thinking their heart's experience, and when they come to the practices of primordial grace, many think their experience of original heart as well. Original heart is not a discrete spiritual event in linear time, but an ongoing blended acknowledgement, and without this experience of blendedness, your practice becomes just another intellectual game in the mind. Original heart is completely, utterly natural, outside the realm of words and concepts. It is experienced directly within the heart if your mind is stepping out of the way and allowing your heart to open. This openness can then touch the heart of the radiance of essence, the timeless aware openness that extends beyond the confines of our being.

When you are centered in the heart's experience of original heart, you will be drawn to the natural world because it resonates with this openness. If you find yourself resistant to being in direct relationship with nature, it is a sign that your mind has hold over your heart, experiencing its own idea of aware openness, and does not want to be challenged. Original heart is the heart and breadth of the radiance of intent arising from essence, it pervades all that naturally arises, a constant tone of experience felt and touched within your heart, expanding beyond self, an expression beyond confinement, a sense of natural freedom.

The Practice of Original Heart

We have emphasized coming to a quality of blended openness naturally within the flow of your experience at first, to avoid the tendency to feel that original heart is something esoteric, separate, or special that must be given to you from outside yourself. The experience of original heart can arise spontaneously within that natural openness in the course of your life and practice, but it is very possible to disregard this subtle change. The mind can so easily be caught up in itself and in maintaining whatever supports its view that it will pass over and dismiss the experience. The luminous aware aspect of your heart has a larger scope beyond the narrow confines of mind: naturally free, unbounded, undefined, sky-like, and clear, an openness with no sense of separate self, touching the continuity of the intent of the essence within the ephemeral arising nature of your experience.

The more you have nurtured the openness of your heart, the more receptive and aware you will be, and you will be spiritually strong enough to stay with the blended acknowledgement of original heart and return to it when your mind has wandered off and clouded your experience. It takes time to gain a heart-based confidence in your ability to return to a genuine experience of original heart. You need to avoid being caught up in a memory of it, or entangled in the mind's concepts about it. You do not want to substitute a memory or a concept for the actual arising experience in the moment, fresh, present, aware. It is crucial to be clear about the difference between a fabricated mental experience and a true acknowledgement of original heart.

Original heart is here, now, one with the fabric of all being, waiting to shine forth once the overlay of societal ignorance, habitual tendencies, and the weighted covers of past actions fade away. A human guide can point out the experience of original heart to you, but this experience also arises naturally within this manifest world. There are countless guides. You can get pointing out from the sky, you can get it from a tree, you can get it from a dewdrop on a leaf, from sunlight on a window sill, from all the myriad expressions of the compassionate intent, wordless, nameless, all around us. And over time this radiant hello will arise more often as you rest within a flow of knowing blended and unconfined. You come back again and again, not through memory but here now, to direct experience of original heart.

The practice of acknowledging and resting in the blended aware spaciousness of original heart, is the practice of not doing anything special, not purifying the world or making it into emptiness or an illusion, just allowing it to be as it is. You sit on the ground outside, sitting in openness with the Earth, as in Earth sitting and return to the expansive connectedness of original heart and remain in that direct experience until your mind wanders off. When it wanders, do not berate yourself, just return and settle within the original heart again. Practicing outdoors with a spacious unobstructed view of the sky can be very helpful at first, but wherever you are, whatever you are doing, you come back again and again. This is the practice. You sit, you stand, you walk, you eat, all the while returning and remaining in original heart. This level of immersion in the practice is best done in long retreat. You need time to settle into the wholeness of the practice to allow a genuine heart confidence to grow, returning to this awareness over and over. It takes much time and practice to become stable, but first you need to be able to return to a clear experience of original heart on your own.

It is very important to be able to settle yourself and return to original heart readily in any situation. All the avenues that we have suggested in the chapter on letting go are valuable supports, Earth walking and sitting on the Earth in wide-angle vision most of all. Returning is not returning to a memory of a previous experience of original heart, or to an idea or concept of it, it is returning to the pure, fresh experience in the moment now, unclouded by judgments or comparisons. Returning is being immersed in a clear pond of aware presence, feeling the luminous intent of the essence reflected in your heart and the heart of all manifestation moving out softly like ripples across the surface of the water.

Being in nature, blending with the natural world, is a powerful support and is essential to re-awakening a subtle awareness of the breadth of all that naturally manifests. To be immersed in the original heart of nature provides a loving embrace for spiritual growth. Immersing yourself, giving yourself to the Earth, living within her embrace, experiencing that loving connection of a Mother's guidance, being within her movement, her firm kindness, allows you to step aside from the mind, and taste the expanse blending your life into what is always there. And when you slip away from original heart, the Earth provides countless ways to let go of the entanglements of mind and rest in an openness that is genuine, a tone of origin. Original heart is the breath of goodness, the fabric of being, a living intent, the path of direct experience, free of the confines of mind.

Three Skies

The three skies practice is a simple and beautiful way to merge into an expansive and fluid experience as a doorway to original heart. In this practice, you blend the clear blue outer sky with the spacious inner sky of your subtle energies and the sky-like quality of your heart. Sit outdoors with a generous view of the sky, settle yourself facing away from the sun and breathe gently with your mouth slightly open. Concentrating on the out breath, pour your heart out softly through your eyes as you pour your breath softly into the blue expanse of space, melding the three skies, giving yourself, surrendering through your eyes and your breath into the generous heart of all being, and then rest in that expanded sphere. You can also do this lying down. Once you have experience with the feeling of the three skies, you can blend them anywhere, even in a small shelter or room.

When your whole being is immersed into the spacious clear presence, you are blended into the sky of blue, the sky of stone, the sky of your body, the sky of insects dancing in the air. The sounds of your mind have subsided into all the skies, the sky of your heart in, around, and within the blue, the blood pulsing, the insects humming. No boundary, no fence, no demarcation, a moment outside time with no way to begin and no point to end, yet livingness, a connection, a heart beat with no rhythm, no melody, no time – a tone unending. A moment of original heart.

This is a practice for when your mind is truly allowing and is not going to break into your experience and make it into its own expression. It is most effective if you have already had years of experience being in wide-angle vision and letting go of habits of perception and identity, and you have a lot of experience sitting within your heart with the Earth, and can acknowledge original heart arising spontaneously.

Sky of Your Heart

All that is touched and touching, breathing in and out of everything else, no separation of kind. All qualities never broken down into compartments of thought, a seamless knowing felt deep in the soul of your heart, the atmosphere of sky filling the unknown knowing of stone, air, water, and fire encompassed within an intent of grace. Feel from an unperceived place in your heart into that knowing unknown, as if standing just outside yourself but all within the expanse of a simple encompassing kindness.

Original heart is an offering, tasting the expanse of all being, simple and unadorned, not attaining a high position in some hierarchy of mind. You come to your birthright that has been long forgotten and is now remembered. You are no more than the stones, wind, plants, and soil that surround you. Original heart is their heart too, you are only coming home. Follow your open heart to this brightness, this luminous open taste of oneness.

As you become aware of the breath of the fabric of being within your daily life, it will change you, it will re-direct your life moving you into closer communion with all that naturally arises from the intent of essence. You are but a breeze within air, now on a fluid trail leading you on a luminous tone poem resolving all that is left of you, just oneness.

Relation

The living experience of original heart is a knowing, primal and ageless, a knowing far beyond the separation, limits, and confinement of cognition. Original heart is a relational knowing beyond the fences and walls put up by the mind. In the practice of original heart, you return to the rhythm of the universe, a primordial simplicity beyond the distinctions, fears, and delusions we have built up to keep us apart.

Within original heart your focus naturally expands to accept the whole beyond self, as an expression of the primal basis of all existence, the fluid, nurturing, expansive, manifesting nature that has no boundaries, the seamless merging of water into water. It is not that we cognitively remember ourselves to be the unity we never left, it is more that separation falls away, for it has never really existed, and only a direct experience of relational wholeness remains, an experience that can be returned to and requires no mediator.

All of our contemporary society is based on structures of separation, the precise and defined mirrors of mind, the limits, rules, boundaries, and hierarchies of all kinds. We must turn from this diseased mind of separation. Let go of all the controls and controllers in order to experience the natural relational wholeness unmarred or undefiled by the mind and its way of corrupting everything it perceives.

Original heart is entering into a true relationship, a direct connection with the intent of essence, a blended being within the movement of all that arises from the radiance of this intent. And in order for those who yearn in their deepest hearts to experience genuine life as origin, we need to live again in full relation within the naturally arising expression of this intent.

The openness and transcendence of original heart are already imbued with the responsibility to relate, a responsibility that requires no one to perceive a need and no need to respond to, only a free movement and a flow of response, a dance in the movement of the fabric of being, a stream flowing, now a pond, now a stream again with the living fluidity of a primal purpose. The relationship of original heart is not a response from one individual being to another; it is a blended presence, a constant responding, with no question or answer, a meeting within being itself.

The movement and flow of response is a transcendent openness within our hearts and the heart of all, a quality of union that has never been separate, only forgotten and then remembered. In true remembrance of relation all walls fall away, all delusional fears are vanquished, and we realize the beatitude of being flowing within and around us, the intent of essence.

Threshing

To hope that you can come to original heart while you are still caught up in and possessed by the lies of mind, hiding from the consequences of our fall from grace, is complete folly. When you are engrossed in delusion, the mind just creates more and more concepts, more diversions from the truth, more ways to tell yourself that you have attained a higher level of being and are part of a great lineage, when in fact, all you have done is pay the rent for the time spent within the walls covered in mirrors reflecting a false dignity as you acquiesce to the lie. Humans of the fall want to be deceived and too often want to deceive themselves and others. True spiritual practice is about seeing clearly, not substituting one lie for another.

Threshing is a practice used in some traditions to help see the difference between the lies of the mind and the clear perception of original heart, but if you have not already come to a true knowing of the difference between heart and mind through direct experience in the natural world, and have not touched that sense of relationship so crucial to original heart, threshing alone will not clarify your experience.

In our times, threshing, also known as *rushan*, has been presented in the West out of context without regard for the necessity of personal experience of living with the Earth as a natural way to open your heart, opening not only to the beings within it but to the whole flow of life that is the natural world. Without this experience, threshing becomes just another mental game. Before the split between heart and mind and the rise of the dominance of the mind, when the natural world was the acknowledged basis of our daily lives, people naturally felt a resonance, a fluid ongoing communication with the myriad lives all around them, not just human. Threshing practice arose within agrarian religious structures that reinforce separation from the natural world and rely primarily on constructed forms of ethical compassion. When practiced with an open heart and a background of direct experience within the natural world, threshing can provide an avenue to connect with the level of empathy and relation that original people lived and moved within naturally.

The threshing practice in its proper context of the vision that is this life can be a dynamic, concentrated experience of touching all life. It requires a decision to leave all that you know and enter the wilderness, not only a wilderness in the physical sense, but also the charnel ground in your heart. It is a commitment to the path beyond promises and vows, a willingness to go anywhere and let go of anything, to go beyond all ordinary experience to follow a spiritual path. Deciding within your heart that you want to reach fruition in this lifetime, being willing to let go of everything that keeps you separate from origin, is a radical step into a deeper level of renunciation and resolve. Something in your heart opens up and demands to return to essence. You let go of all that hinders you, and there is a profound freedom in reaching this threshold. This freedom of heart mirrors itself in untouched wilderness or other places of solitude, danger, beauty, and grace, like the charnel grounds of old, and in this free space, you do the threshing practice to clarify your relationship to all life, the radiant intent of the essence.

Threshing is a process of separating two things that have been mixed together, in the most literal sense separating chaff from seed. The threshing practice is a way to see the difference between heart and mind through the eyes of myriad beings whether they are caught in separate identity or more open within the pure experience of original heart. Go into the wilderness alone and find a secluded place far from people. Strip naked, and for two, three, or four days, take on the actions, sounds, and feelings of all beings in all aspects of this arising vision as they come to you, one after another. In our times, designated wilderness areas are often high use areas, so you may need to find a wilderness that is on private land to be sure that you will not be seen, heard, or interrupted in your practice.

Once you have chosen a site for your practice, sit quietly and pray. Ask the beings, spirits, and elementals that live in the area to help you. Make offerings. Open your heart to the holy ones and all creation. Dedicate your life and the practice you are about to do as a prayer that all life may live in harmony with the intent of essence. Then sit quietly and enter into a moment in some other being's life, making it real, vivid, and detailed. Sometimes you enter the vividness using all the senses available to your imagination, at other times take on the actual sounds and actions with your body. Either way, allow whatever arises, good, bad, probable or improbable, from any realm of being into your experience, allow it to become very visceral, bring it to life. Once you really feel that you are fully inside that being's experience, stop the experience, drop into your heart, drop into original heart and settle right where and how you are. Without any preconceptions, let your heart be open and free. Then after a short time, allow another moment of·another being's life to arise within you and repeat the process.

Ever since humans turned away from a blended existence with the Earth and the fabric of being, separation has become the norm and realms of aberration have taken their place. There are countless realms of experience within this world, both positive and negative, and you have probably touched or felt many of them in the course of your life: the endless hostility and strife of explosive anger; the rigidity and resentment of old, deeply held angers; the desperation of longing and grasping; the dullness, dangers, and comforts of habits; the tensions of hopes and fears and choices; the strain of jealousy and greed; and the numbing bliss and pride of self-absorption. In the practice of threshing, the emphasis is generally on returning to original heart from the confined states of various negative emotions and mind, but do not forget to touch the positive aspects of all life as well: the generosity of selfless love, gestures of true nurturing, and moments of innocent wonder, in human, animal, plant, or elemental form. Let them all arise naturally and freely in no particular order.

As you take on the identities of countless diverse beings, their responses and motivations, the demands of their hopes, fears, joys, and angers, you are wearing away at the tenacity of your personal experience, the continuity of your habits of mind and emotions. You wear away the last strongholds of these habitual tendencies, the holding to what you know and the fascination with your personal drama. You see through the dreams of beings lost in their obscurations; you see what keeps them from a pure experience of oneness, and how separate they have become from our Mother Earth and what keeps them from fruition. Stepping outside yourself and entering the identity of others, feeling their sufferings and joys as if they were your own, widens the scope of your heart and deepens your compassion and sense of oneness with all beings. You see the ghost-like nature of all identity, including your own, and you know without a doubt that all experience is an expression of the great compassion and love of the intent of essence letting you and every being see the fruit of your intentions and habits, teaching you, guiding you, calling you to return to origin.

As you enter into the threshing experiences, making them as vivid and real as you can, you are also activating your own dynamic creative energy, the spontaneously arising fertile power of the essence within you. The primordial visions of light are the purest expression of the dynamic energy of the essence, and you need to allow and recognize that same aspect within your own energies in order to meet the visions. Because the practice of the visions of radiance also greatly amplifies the dynamic quality of your personal experience, you need to learn how to stay open to it, to allow it and not hold to it at the same time, to learn how to orient yourself within this fluid wash of organic being.

Threshing practice is a sacred offering, a prayer. As you step outside yourself, taking on the habits of others without judgments, likes, or dislike, touching spontaneous presence directly in the free play of your imagination, you see that all identities are like cloaks we wear, shells, chaff, the outer coverings of a deeper energy. You see clearly the vividness and the molten force hidden within the structures of this or any life. The point of threshing is not to play out desires, fantasies, or fears but to recognize the process by which all experience arises, to free the dynamic potential of your experience so that you can give your whole being into the practice of the visions of radiance. How well threshing does this depends on how much work you have done before. As with any spiritual practice, threshing is only as effective as what you bring to it, particularly your level of renunciation and your experience of the vision that is this life as an expression of the intent of the essence and the widening scope of your heart opening to that intent.

On the last day of your threshing retreat spend a few hours as a *corpse* for each day you spent embodying the realms, a half day of the corpse for three and half days of threshing and so forth. The corpse practice calms and restores your subtle energies after you have completed threshing. Become the physical body after death. Lie perfectly still with no ability or necessity to move, no need to sleep or eat or defend or take care of anything. Your only function is to dissolve, to surrender to the physical forces of decay as the elements of your body naturally fall away.

Earth Refuge

Refugia: areas that can allow organisms to survive times of adverse environmental/social conditions.
Relict: a species that was once widespread that survives in small groups and areas.

Earth refuge in original heart is a transformative creative process defined only by what naturally arises, an ongoing active play of openness, fluidity, expansiveness, and nurturing. Within the natural improvisation of the arising improvisation of the vision that is this life, everything moving together, heart to heart within the moment, fluidly, spontaneously, you move organically on a path of openness and transcendence, always moving toward oneness, a reunion with origin.

But spiritual followers of the heart are now facing the challenges of a spiritual path at a time when our planet is in crisis and humanity is falling deeper into madness. Times such as these require special acts or gestures of the heart to oppose and survive the senseless insane acts of our species. Gestures that are inherent to the blessing and grace within all life are prayers that a kinder future could still arise out of the ashes of this madness. An Earth refuge is such a gesture. Its ability to affect change does not have to be shown to the world or witnessed by anyone, for its rings of truth reverberate through the universe touching all things, a rippling flow of bright purpose and prayer, returning to a life within original heart as naturally as a stone falling into a pond spreading rings across the surface of the water.

The basic structure and activity of an Earth refuge is to return to the openness and fluidity of original heart. The practice is to blend with original heart at all times of the day and night, without trying or thinking it, entering into a fluid relation with the moment by moment manifestation of life, returning to the natural flow and rhythm of the heart. The prayer is living the purpose day and night in the loving experience of the path. The ritual is taking each breath, each step, toward a blended acknowledgement. The ceremony is the circle, the people of the heart, caring for the same purpose and intent, a solitude and an embrace, both personal and all encompassing. The instruction is the intent of essence manifesting as the natural world, and all that naturally arises within the vision of life is the boundary, a boundary that extends without limits.

A spiritual life with the Earth is a life lived within original heart as a blended heart to heart relation with our Mother Earth, reclaiming a fluid openness, a knowing beyond cognition, an atmosphere without boundaries, an expansion beyond progress and space, a love within an empowered intent, and living in an Earth shelter is a vital support for the intent of this path. Simple shelters built with natural materials bermed with earth allow you to live and practice

171

surrounded by the Earth's absorbing depth and nurturing power. These dwellings are cool in summer, warm in winter, and grounded both physically and spiritually. They are built on good spots that are welcoming and suitably spaced apart from one another to allow each member of the retreat community privacy and direct relationship with the plants, birds, insects, animals, reptiles, and elementals all around them, and with the Earth herself, all as family.

In an Earth refuge, small groups of followers of the heart support each other's spiritual prayer toward a blended existence. We come together to grow our own food and help each other in the building and repairing of our shelters, looking after each other when we are sick, creating a circle of intent, making sure we all have enough to support our ongoing journey to a true embrace. We become the prayer of Earth and heart even while we experience the dimming in our times of the heartbeat of our First Mother. An Earth refuge is a prayer of return to the origin of heart, and a prayer that the heartbeat of the Earth may grow strong again.

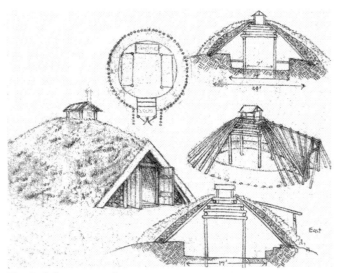

Earth shelter construction

An Earth refuge is a personal relationship with the Earth and the sacred intent of essence, a relationship that affects everything about your spiritual life including how and where you build your shelter depending on what the land naturally offers. Here we are including some selections from our memoir about setting up our retreat in the mountains of northern California as an example.

We were overjoyed to be going into retreat at last. During the coming weeks, we searched the mountain when we could get the time. The land was very steep, and it was hard to find a small knoll that shed water on all four sides. We finally found a site, a twenty-five-minute hike uphill from the Gonpa, on a small, nearly

173

level terrace of mostly madrone and fir. Through the screen of trees growing on the steeper slope below and the tall trunks of trees closer around us, the gray and brown furrowed columns of Douglas fir and the curving red-barked muscular shapes of madrone, we could see small patches of brightness from the sky and the narrow river valley farther below. It was not exactly an overlook, but there was a gentler opening here, a place where we felt the elementals were inviting us to stay, and we prayed for this land and our retreat, feeling a sense of blessing, an auspicious warmth surrounding us. We explored further, and a quarter mile down an old deer trail we found a hidden area along a small creek that had escaped the damage of the mining and logging years, a healing fertile place with stands of horsetail, wild ginger, and other medicinal plants under grand old moss-covered maples and oaks where we could go for water each day.

We moved up the mountain in mid-August, pitched a small backpacking tent, and started digging. We dug down two and half feet when we hit a hard layer of shale, so we modified our design and built a pit dwelling instead, half in and half out of the earth. The circular hole was fourteen feet across. In the center we set four posts, seven feet apart and seven feet high, and joined them with more beams, creating a square frame with a tapering chimney shape above. We laid long peeled poles against the frame in a circle, making a low teepee shape that extended three feet past the excavated area on all sides. Then we tacked peeled branches around the outside of the poles, making a kind of basket, leaving a smoke hole in the center. Since there was no appropriate supply of bark here to use for the roof, we added a layer of black plastic. We bermed the outside with all the earth we had dug out of the hole and heaped a thick layer of fallen leaves, twigs, and small branches over the earth. We had built a cave.

During the day there was always a soft light from the smoke hole, and in the warm glow of candle light at night, the peeled poles were like golden rays pouring down from the center of the roof. Even the black plastic had a beauty then, like the night sky showing between the branches and the beams. The air moved through the space from two small screened openings above the door up to the smoke hole and later a screened cupola. It was a tight fit but we had room for a shrine, a cot-like bed for each of us to sleep and practice on, an earthen shelf all around for our belongings stored in plastic bins, and eventually a tiny woodstove in the center. Within the protective insulating layers of forest debris and earth, the shelter was comfortable enough, shed rain, and held the steady temperatures of the earth, cool in summer, warm in winter, never dropping below fifty-two degrees. In order to keep our animal and insect house guests to a minimum, we cooked under a tarp a good distance away. Beyond our future tiny woodstove, the only modern convenience in the shelter was a four-foot-tall hinged door. The round domed shape with a low entryway to the east reminded us of the turtle in the Pine Barrens. We were home.

Our Earth shelter blended into the forest

We knew that this time of spiritual refuge was our way to the complete path of original heart and the visions of radiance. Here was our pathway to the sacred where we could open within the heart of the Earth. It was a place of return to origin, a place to nourish ourselves, to delve within and allow ourselves to open to the full scope of primordial grace.

We were grateful we had taken the time to learn traditional ways of living with the Earth, embracing the knowledge that we are one with the Earth and we could abide with her, letting go of the fear that holds contemporary man apart. We felt a freedom within our daily lives from knowing we were an aspect of this natural wholeness, something the yogis of old who practiced in the wilderness or charnel grounds would have been familiar with since childhood.

We were still confronted by the growing catastrophe of our modern world; the solitude and practice only made us more sensitive to it. It was close by, in the ongoing reverberation of trucks, cars, and motorcycles echoing along the highway on the other side of the river in this narrow valley, a constant reminder of the insanity and suffering of our times.

The word "retreat" often used for spiritual time apart can be misleading. Withdrawal, defeat and avoidance of difficulty or danger are listed first in the dictionary before the meanings of seclusion, reflection and prayer, and none of these definitions come close to evoking the dynamic, intense process that a true Earth refuge entails.

It was understood that the boundaries for our refuge included staying "in" for as long as it took to reach the fruition of the path. We rarely left the land, except for a few teachings and for medical emergencies. There was a tangible support in our energetic bond with the Earth in this place, the knoll, the shelter, the creek, the trail we took to get water, and with our practice, a visceral elastic force, an intent to complete the path. There was a support of another kind in the sameness and simplicity of the days, boundaries in time as well as space. We would get up very early before dawn for a full practice session before breakfast, have a second long session before lunch, do a few chores after lunch as needed, then another session in the late afternoon, followed by a light meal and a longer session into the night. We would rise early and begin again, with no vacations, no holidays, no weekends, and no days off.

This was the basic schedule of our days, but there is a fine art to shaping your practice in a spiritual refuge. When you sit, you need to be both unmoving and relaxed. The tension of rigidity is a movement of its own, a constant holding to the inverse of movement. The way you shape your time is similar; extreme punctuality can be as much of a distraction as laziness. Just as in the studio when we were artists, we were here for an intent we were following deep in our hearts. That was the compass point, the guiding force. Everything else falls into place in relation to that overriding purpose, the burning need to acknowledge and return to the utter completeness of essence.

All the daily routines and practices can open into a spaciousness unseen before, but the process can also be hard, tedious work. Your habits and emotions are all there, along with ailments, illnesses, and upwellings of subtle energy. These and other difficult experiences can arise for you, not against you, to help you on the path, when you see firsthand how much it is the holding, grasping, and denial that imprison you, not the difficulties themselves, and you let go. This is the crucial shift, the gap that allows a spacious open heart to become more evident, sky-like, yet filled with intrinsic grace.

We were both middle aged when we entered retreat, and we knew this was our last chance. Hauling water or supplies in the rain, even when we were sick or tired, we still had to go uphill yet again. We just kept going. The simplicity of our life, uncluttered and lean, was the ground, the basis on which we placed our practice, and the constant presence of the forest, the Earth, the rain, the simple tasks, became not only a strength encouraging us along the path, but a natural reflection of the practice itself.

We were choosing to do all this. This was the way the opportunity to immerse ourselves in the path had arisen for us, and our hearts were grateful beyond measure, even though our bodies at times found it hard to haul food buckets out to the kitchen tarp again, setting up for the third meal of the day in freezing pouring rain. You can experience the absence of modern comforts in so many ways, and that discontinuity, held within the structure of your refuge, steadily transforms every moment, every aspect of your life, your relations with your family, your memories, your pain and frustrations, everything. Our difficulties did not have the exhilarating drama or beauty of being snowbound on a high mountain. We were faced instead with gray skies and rain, and the mildew, mold, and damp of a forest enclosure as a context for the final stage of our long process of letting go. The hardest part was being cut off from the sky, but even that became at last saturated with true joy, a quiet wild delight rooted in the very essence of being, as we found the sky-like freedom we sought in our practice instead.

PART II

The Visionary
Path of Radiance

Please respect this text. You hold in your hands a doorway to a sacred primordial practice, a connection to nameless holy ones who have accomplished this path. Do not practice the path of radiance until you are able to acknowledge original heart, for the path will not unfold in an authentic way without this crucial acknowledgement. Please do not teach or guide anyone in the visionary practice of radiance until you have completed the four visions of this path.

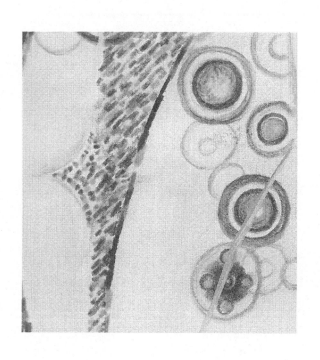

Primordial Joy

Bubbles form all across the still pond in a light rain. They arise suddenly, and linger for a while. Some mass together while others drift away. Rainbow colors swirl across their fragile curves becoming more and more delicate, becoming luminous nets growing thinner and thinner until they burst, temporary structures of time and space returning just as suddenly as they appeared, essence, sphere, essence.

After following a path of letting go, learning the way of an open heart and an allowing mind, and acknowledging original heart, you come to a beginning, a threshold. The seed in your heart initiates the ripening of your path through the visionary practice of radiance. It is as if you become a sphere riding upon the essence, becoming less and less held by time, space, shape, and distance, more and more a unity beyond separation, a unity of all experience, all phenomena, that resolves in an instant, essence, essence, essence.

The visionary path of radiance is a path of return from the point of origin, just as a circle is drawn. In the movement of a line sweeping around and curving back to merge seamlessly with itself, completion is inherent in the path from the beginning. The whole process of reunion with origin is all around us reflected in the natural world, infinitely patiently teaching us to acknowledge our place within its embrace. Circles and the movement of return to origin are expressions of the cyclical nature of the radiance of the essence that weaves the entire world experience we find ourselves within. They are the basis for the path of radiance, and they shape all manifestation, from atoms and molecules and the orbits of subatomic particles, to planets and stars and the dance of their movements within the larger movements of the universe itself.

Circles and cycles from the point of origin are apparent everywhere. Bubbles form and disappear on water in a light rain; rainbows bloom in a misty sky; seeds sprout, grow upward, mature and set seed again; waters flow in rivulets and mountain streams into larger rivers leading to the sea, then rise into sky and clouds, and fall as rain on mountaintops again. A luminous seed or sphere of this sacred cycle is in the heart of every being, waiting to be awakened and return you to the essence through the visions of radiance, a spontaneous, dynamic visionary process arising from your heart and the very basis of all experience. The visions are a coherent message of divine intent, arising in the same way and in the same progression for everyone. They are the primordial birthright of all beings, a profound connection with the essence manifest in its purest form. Suffused with the pure joy of becoming, they offer a natural, unconfused path free of the assumptions of language or culture, and the four great visions of radiance become your teacher just as the Earth has been your teacher since birth, through direct experience of the heart.

On this primordial path, you rest in original heart, settle your body and eyes in specific postures and gazes and breathe in a specific way, to open a very subtle channel that leads from your heart to your eyes. Nourished by the soil of your heart that you have prepared through all the previous practices, the luminous seed in your heart opens and begins to grow upward toward your eyes, giving rise to the fluid ongoing experience called the four visions.

The visions of radiance lead you to oneness through the guiding field of spontaneous presence, an actual relationship with the radiance of the essence. It is an experience of total joy. Settled in original heart, perceiving the seed of light and knowing in your heart that you are immersed in the direct perception of the holy ones, you enter the final path, a path of living light at the very edge of the essence, the point of origin, a sacred, joyous knowing.

The holy ones before the fall, followed the signs and cycles of Earth, water and sky, moon and sun, seed to seed. They found the luminous seed in their hearts through the vision that is this life, through the rays of the sun, the water of their eyes, and the light of their hearts. They watched, they waited, they allowed; they followed their hearts without hurrying, following the intent of the essence, allowing the visions of radiance. When you live in acknowledgement with the fabric of being and gaze within the embrace of the visions, you are joining all the holy ones throughout time and space and beyond who have brought the four visions to consummation. You are joined within the embrace of the same visions, the same radiance. Your heart blends with the hearts of the holy ones and the heart of all, your practice is a living prayer joined with their prayers.

Inner Radiance

Inner radiance is a deeper experience of the natural luminosity of your heart. It is the intent of the essence within your heart blossoming, opening beyond thought or description, fluid, molten, luminous joy, evanescent yet palpable, arising as anything and everything, from the shining dewdrop on a leaf in the early morning to the light of your own heart. Inner radiance is the moon in a clear sky before dawn, the translucent illumined stems and leaves of a young plant, the shining rainbow, and the iridescent body of an emerging cicada. It is a heightened experience of the original heart spreading out of your heart like light across the sky with an innocent joy.

As your practice of returning to original heart deepens, inner radiance begins to blossom naturally, expanding, pushing outward, until, like the calyx around the new bud of a flower, the husk of your ignorance cracks open and allows this glory of inner light to appear, the natural response of a clear and luminous heart. In those moments as inner radiance dawns, it opens like a flower both within your heart and within the world, a glory of oneness, the effulgence of an inner light, open and gentle, receptive to all. Restrictions fall away, only the subtle light of one's heart remains suffusing and arising out of all that you perceive.

To allow the very the fabric of being to guide you, you must be able to allow and then surrender completely to the guiding force of this light within your heart.

Sacred Demand

Returning to original heart takes you to the natural expansiveness within your familiar experience. The visionary path of radiance shifts your experience entirely. Slowly, gently, quietly, steadily, the unfolding visions literally go beyond all experience, taking as the path the manifesting energy of the essence itself, transforming your very being.

You need to be sure that you have prepared the ground and nurtured the soil of your heart before you proceed with this path. To allow the visions to arise naturally, you need to embrace the Earth in your heart. You need to become Earth, receptive, accepting, humble, and devoted, to join with the holy ones. It is crucial that you experience original heart in relation to the natural world, as an engaged openness from your heart, not as a construct of mind, for the visions to arise in an authentic way. The path of radiance is not about holding to or generating an image. The visions of radiance are not mind experiences or visualizations; they are direct perception of the radiance of essence. The process is not an experience based on fine points of doctrine, nor is it grasping at whatever comes up in the practice or your mind. You need to know the difference between mind and heart and to have taken responsibility for your spiritual path. If you have a human guide who has completed the path of radiance from a heart perspective, you can receive their view on whether it is time to proceed with this path. Very likely during the end of this age and the coming of the next you will be on your own, hopefully holding this book. The knowing and the blessings will come to you, guiding you to the final resolution.

The path of radiance is about entering into a relational embrace with living light, becoming fully engaged with the visions, and the intent within the radiance becomes your teacher guiding you to essence. This is a path of no doubts. A wordless knowing dawns in your heart that this living intent suffuses all life including your own heart, and that you can reach fruition in this life.

Once the heart seed initiates the cycle of the four visions, the growth of the visions is very similar to the way a seed sprouts in nutrient-rich soil and rises up out of the ground. When one has come to genuine humbleness, renunciation, and an open heart and an allowing mind, there is a potential developing within one's heart seed. The seed of light quickens with an energy delicate yet endowed with the strength to push upward toward the portal where the visions become evident. The seedling of light rises out of all your renunciation, openness, and fluidity, your love and compassion, which then nourish its growth. Subtle, soft, allowing, gentle wonder as grace itself takes you along the path. The visions of radiance are a living, evolving cycle that needs to be nurtured; you need to give everything to the practice to keep it going. This requires being in long-term retreat. If the visions begin to arise, they are a sacred demand. A very rare and precious gift is opening in your heart. Do not take it lightly.

Not everyone is called to the path of the radiance. When one is truly called from their deepest heart to be immersed in the ineffable grace of blending with essence, completely erased in the oneness at the origin of all, you will be willing to give up anything, all rank or power, all badges of identity, willing to die if necessary to live this path. This is a mystic's way, the path of blending your all into the great heart of all. It is the natural path already laid out in the heart of all creation, not a path of mind and power but the path of love and the openness of interrelation of which every one of us, aware or not, is already a part. And the particular joy of this path is the immensity of the beauty and the love with which you are welcomed home.

Colors

The curtain of rain moved east at sunset. Clouds opened in the west to allow the last rays of the sun to bless the land. A vivid rainbow suddenly appeared glowing in the moist gray air, and then a second rainbow slowly melted into view above the first. Two perfect arches soared huge across the sky, their bands of color luminous in the soft twilight. Transparent lines of delicate pink and turquoise rippled on the underside of the inner arch, echoes of another grace, the rainbow's inner life. Thick gray clouds behind the double rainbow began to pull apart, revealing a deep clear cobalt blue, vibrant, self-luminous, enfolding all the east, dissolving distant mountains and evening sky into the same blue radiance.

The essence encompasses all being; there is nothing that is not the essence. The essence abides as the blue-black depth of all and the glowing cobalt of the twilight sky, nothing not nothing, pure primordial potential arising spontaneously as the colors of the rainbow and the light that manifests all appearances, all phenomena that we experience in our lives. The cobalt, cerulean, and ultramarine of the sky, the gray pearlescent mists of clouds, the moist or dry touch of the air, the gentle or fierce heat of the sun, are all woven in increasingly complex patterns of the elemental colors themselves.

Red-orange-yellow, white-green-blue, indigo-violet-lavender, dawn pink, sky blue, the faint turquoise depths of clear water, colors upon colors unfold as sacred elements, Earth, air, water, fire, and space, as sacred directions north, south, east, west, center, above, below. From the grand cardinal energies of this shared vision we call life to the minutest detail, everything is born of and saturated with living light, a message of primordial intent that surrounds us in the natural world and can be read deep within our hearts.

Many cultures recognize the sacred nature of directions, colors, and the basic elements. The maps may differ because of local landscape and position on the globe of the Earth, but they all reflect acknowledgement of a natural holy power, a guiding force, the sacred compass within which we live. This entire world experience contains all the holy qualities. You can follow them back to the essence, learn from them within your own heart, and through the visions of radiance, you come to see and experience directly this fundamental organization and shape of our world as a mandala of five spheres of color, four around a central sphere.

This equal cross arrangement represents the very basis of emanation in which colors, elements, and directions are arranged naturally as a wholeness, a union beyond separation, but within this dynamic equilibrium five clearly distinguishable colors are sometimes singled out as organizing factors for a variety of qualities. They are sometimes presented as aids for refining your acknowledgement of five qualities of inner radiance. In this grouping of colors, they are used as a way to become aware of the mind's tendency to grab onto and inhibit the genuine experience of original heart, preventing it from blossoming into inner radiance.

In the visions of radiance, the range of color is much more dynamic, and there are literally oceans of qualities that arise from your heart outside of categorization. We offer this list as a starting point for recognizing not only the pitfalls of how your mind can affect your experience of original heart and inner radiance, but also for recognizing the generative power of colors themselves outside classifications and systems. The presence and qualities of color can also be experienced directly in the natural world. Warm colors come forward and engage, while cooler colors soothe and allow a sense of space, as in the blue of sky and distance. Green heals, and is the color of the life force of the plants, and so forth.

Red

The color red is associated with the element fire. The radiant nature of red and fire kindles and enlivens, from the red blood cells in our bodies to the glowing warmth of a campfire, and it inspires and brings creativity and meditative bliss. Red is the aspect of radiance that illuminates and appreciates the myriad forms of manifestation but does not get lost in the details. If the mind grabs on to this breadth of perception, it corrupts this energy into the grasping and holding of desire.

Yellow-Gold

The color yellow-gold is associated with the element Earth. The radiant nature of yellow-gold and Earth is balancing; from the golds of harvest grains and sunlight to the richness of butter and egg yolks, it nurtures and increases positive qualities, creating an interconnected abundance in which everything is equal. Yellow-gold is the aspect of radiance that is an expression of the groundedness and stability of oneness. If the mind grasps on to this generosity of perception, it becomes caught in jealousy.

White

The color white is associated with the element water. Like a vast lake, the radiant nature of white and water is lucid, fluid, calm, and reflective. White is the openness of radiance, reflecting clearly whatever appears before it, yet it is not disturbed by the reflections. When the mind intrudes with its partisan views, the lucid mirroring quality of water and white is dulled, clouded, and disturbed, and the mind can solidify the experience into anger and resentment.

Green

The color green is associated with the element wind. The radiant nature of green and wind is movement, fresh, quick, active, and alive. The green of chlorophyll literally supports all life and growth on the Earth. Green is the manifesting aspect of radiance. If the mind appropriates this manifesting energy for itself, it falls to pride, identification with the doer and the effort of doing rather than seeing that everything is spontaneously arising, already accomplished moment by moment.

Blue

The color blue is associated with the element of space. The radiant nature of blue and space is expansive, vast, and all encompassing, from the blues of the sky to the hues of distant mountains and the depths of the sea. Blue is the aspect of radiance that is the knowingless knowing of oneness. If this expansive all-encompassing quality is not recognized and accepted by the mind, the mind will dominate over the heart and remain enmeshed in ignorance, expressed as the familiar limitations of holding to separate identity.

When you are in the visions of radiance, you come to deeper and deeper experience of the radiance of color, this primordial expression of the intent of essence. The colors seen in the visions are more than optical phenomena, or symbols or overlays. Colors are alive outside sets of five, outside all categories, with a quality to their aliveness that is beyond ordinary perception. Through the visions as you move closer and closer to the essence, you see them directly just as they are, elemental forces, the actual fabric of being, beyond concepts of space and time.

Heartlamps and Pathways

The basic instructions for the visionary practice of radiance are grouped as heartlamps and pathways. They are recognitions and techniques that you rely on to guide and illuminate your experience. The first three heartlamps are the basis of how the visions arise. The pathways are the methods that support and facilitate the practice. The second group of heartlamps clarifies the actual practice, and we introduce them later, after the sections on gazing.

Heartlamp of the Heart Seed

The visions of radiance arise from a luminous seed in your heart, the intent of essence that is present in all that naturally arises as a seed of living light. The heart seed is a gift within a gift, like the sun, the sky, the eyes, the openness of your heart, and the radiance of a candle flame, all manifesting a sublime path to this grace of return to origin already in your heart.

Through the path of original heart and Earth, you kindle this seed, which initiates the cycle of the four visions on the visionary path of radiance. In the practice of the visions, the sacred intent within the heart seed arises as rainbow colored circles and rosaries of light, bodily forms of the deities and the holy ones, and other expressions of the visions, blending with you, purifying your very being. The visions are a fluidity beyond coming or going, a vast sea of manifest forms of light reflecting out of your heart. This immense array already present within your heart, the essence already abiding within you as the luminous holy forms alight with grace, is the *heartlamp of the heart seed.*

Heartlamp of the Channel of Light

Like a slender hollow silken thread or a very fine strand of fiber optic cable, *the channel of light* rises from the heart, curves upward to the crown chakra at the top of the head and descends to the eyes where it divides in two and moves outward through each eye, spreading and curving gently. This is not one of the channels of energy associated with the chakras, but a particular channel through which the radiance manifests in direct perception as the four visions. The kindled light of the heart seed rises like the arched neck and stem of a young seedling pushing up through the soil to lift the leaves, and gives rise to the channel of light and the special subtle energy that moves within this channel allowing the luminous visions to flow from the heart to the eyes. This energy of living light, the pure subtle energy of the essence and the channel together form *the heartlamp of the channel of light.*

Heartlamp of the Eyes

The fluid receptive nature of the eyes and their ability to perceive light is called the *heartlamp of the eyes*. The eye has a natural fluid power that reaches out and connects with what it sees, and has sometimes been called a *water lasso* for that reason. The eyes can meet, hold, push, or pull at need. If this power is guided by the mind, the mind grabs onto what the eyes see, and pulls it back into itself and interprets it in ways that reinforce perceptions upholding separate identity. The eyes can also be used more purely, to connect with and relate, and with this more open use of the eyes, you bond and blend with the visions as they arise. Then the lasso quality becomes a mutual embrace, as you embrace the visions and are embraced by them.

The physical eye is a miraculous organ, a vast realm of elemental forces of water and light. Light passes through this living sea going both ways, from the heart and from the outside. Outer light and inner light meet in the water of the eye. Elemental water serpent *naga* energies are traditionally associated with this primordial power of water and eyes that supports the arising of the visionary process in your experience.

In the practice of radiance, perceiving the visions involves the dynamics between three aspects of seeing: the physical eye, visual processing by the brain, and original heart. As you practice, the heart connects directly with the eyes, bypassing the interpretations laid on visual experience by the mind and you see directly with the eyes of the heart.

Current science has come to understand the complex dynamics of sight in ways that clarify this key aspect of the practice. The retina has an intelligence of its own that processes incoming visual images for color, outline, and motion before sending them to the brain. In ordinary sight, the brain processes the images for distance, dimension, and detail, assigns meaning, and consolidates the information into the visual perceptions we are accustomed to seeing. The brain greatly enhances the images sent by the retina so we rarely see what the retina actually sees. Nerve cells in part of the pineal gland contain a pigment similar to the pigment of the retina. This organ associated with the crown chakra is a remnant of an ancient eye, and still governs multiple perceptions, including bodily rhythm and equilibrium as well as perception of light through the skin and eyes. The route of the channel of light, curving upward through the crown chakra and down again toward the eyes, provides a vital support for the retina seeing in its own way as an alternative to seeing primarily with the habitual patterns of mind and subtle energy, which helps free the eyes to go beyond ordinary patterns of perception, allowing the dimensionless visions to unfold.

Most people have allowed their mind to be dominant and use their eyes in a channeled, tunnel vision way, grabbing blindly out of the negative emotions and limitations of separate identity. If you do not break from this narrow grabbing action, the four visions will not unfold in an authentic way. Your experience of the visions will be distorted and perceived according to the mind's expectations, and you will never see what the retina sees, never see clearly with the eyes of the heart. You will see what the mind wants to see and be cut off from the full generative transforming power of the visions themselves. Visualization practices further reinforce and accentuate channeled holding by the visual mind, and practitioners of paths that emphasize visualization face a considerable challenge if they are called to the path of radiance. They will need to spend time reorienting to the way of the heart if they are to overcome the patterns and neural pathways of inner tunnel vision set up by their previous practice.

The eyes and the heart and eye connection are such a defining aspect of the path of radiance that the practice is often referred to as *gazing* by practitioners, and so it is absolutely crucial to come to this path with eyes already aligned with your heart. Blindfolded walking with wide-angle vision can help release the hold that the brain or the mind has on the retina and allow the heart to unfold. Sitting and waiting quietly for animals, keeping your eyes in wide-angle vision as an animal comes closer, is also good training for recognizing the power of your eyes and how you are using them. As we mentioned earlier in the section on letting go, animals will feel the quality of your eyes, and they will bolt if your eyes grab onto to them and so will the visions of radiance. If you have already trained in blindfolded walking and waiting for animals, you have a good start for your eyes to gaze with reverent, allowing openness, blending with the visions welling up from within your heart through the channel of light.

Pathway of the Postures

There are three postures specific to the practice. Each posture has a quality that supports your practice in a different way, and the postures have traditional names that evoke the ways they align your body to the practice. Train in these postures until you can sit in one of them for hours at a time without moving.

In the *posture of the lion*, you sit with the alert regal bearing of a seated lion, upright with the soles of your feet together close in front of you and your knees out to the sides. Your back is straight, you gaze with your head slightly tilted upward looking just above the horizon. Your arms are straight, and your hands are placed in front of you, either beside or in front of your feet, or behind your feet depending on how close you can bring your feet to your body. Your fingers wrap around your thumbs making fists like lion paws. The lion posture raises energy up through your body and has a transcendent quality.

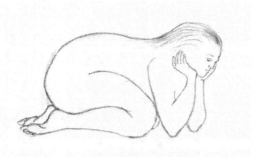

In the *posture of a sleeping elephant,* you kneel with your body curled up like the huge bulk of an elephant resting completely at ease on a vast shore of an inner sea. You crouch on your knees, elbows touching the ground, hands supporting your chin, with your feet together with toes pointing back. Your abdomen presses on your upper thighs. You gaze slightly to the side, either right or left, like an archer sighting down an arrow. The elephant posture brings a quality of inner heat and bliss, mellowing, soothing your energy.

In the *posture of the mountain yogi,* you sit on the Earth in openness, unencumbered, stable, and balanced, with your feet flat on the ground, your back straight, and your knees drawn up to your chest. Your abdomen is held in slightly toward your spine, and you pull up slightly on the perineum, the lower door. Your arms are folded with your left elbow on your left knee and your left hand on your right knee. Your right arm is on top, with the right elbow on top of the left hand, and the right hand on top of the left elbow. This cools heat

in the body. There are alternative hand and arm positions. Resting your elbows on your knees with hands supporting your chin balances heat and cold. Crossing your arms with your hands in the opposite arm pits raises heat if you are cold. You gaze looking downward within a sense of balance and stability that supports openness. For any of the mountain yogi postures, you need to support your back with a meditation belt, a strong soft band four to eight inches wide that encircles your body just below your knees, supports your back. This will hold your knees comfortably close to your chest. You might also find it helpful to sit on a thick firm cushion with your feet a little lower flat on the ground. The mountain yogi posture evens your energy and supports resting in original heart.

The postures allow you to remain motionless for hours and align your body and subtle energies in a way that supports the unfolding of the visions. They are crucial to the practice. The lion, the elephant, and the mountain yogi are the three main postures, and whichever one you use at any given time depends on your subtle energy, how the visions are arising, the weather, time of day or night, and so forth. Practice in each of these postures so that you become comfortable in them and can stay in one of them for a long time without moving. The qualities of transcendence, bliss, stability, and so forth attributed to the postures are not so defined in practice. You can touch all of these qualities within any posture but each posture does have specific effects on your personal energies, enlivening, soothing, or balancing, and you may find that you have an affinity for one of them and will want to spend most of your time in that posture.

Pathway of the Breath

Go into silence and harness the energy of your breath by breathing gently through the mouth with your lips slightly open, pausing on the out breath, then breathing in again softly through the mouth, elongating the out breath on each cycle. Emphasizing the out breath supports receptive energy and helps you come into the blending, merging quality of gazing.

Train in this gentle breathing through the mouth and pausing on the out breath until it becomes natural, flowing, easy, and smooth. Through this breathing, you are drawing closer to the subtle resonance of the Earth, and as your breathing slows, it can stop spontaneously as the resonance deepens. The more you breathe in this way, the more your subtle energy calms down and the more the display of the vision slows down and becomes more stable. Give up all speech, including chanting and prayers, even silently, as in a vision quest. Gazing is a primordial form of communication and prayer in itself, so allow the offering to unfold. Also give up any exercise that will activate or increase your subtle energy. Both the breathing and the silence help the more subtle winds subside and you do not want to stir the winds up again with other practices.

Pathway of the Heart

Gaze without wavering. Pour your heart, your attention, and your breath into the embrace of the vision. Do not indulge in concepts or speculation about the visions. Just rest your gaze in an open, allowing way, melting into and blending with the visions, the natural luminosity of the essence.

In the complete path of primordial grace, you first come to acknowledge, return to, and remain in original heart at will, and then you enter the path of radiance. If you have an open heart and an allowing mind, then even if your practice of original heart is not yet stable, you will experience deeper qualities of original heart directly through the visions, and this will lead you to more stable experience. At first, it can be difficult to settle in the dynamic quality of inner radiance arising as the visions. The practice will amplify every aspect of your mind. You will feel its naturally molten and effulgent qualities far more than in other forms of spiritual practice. If you are still holding and grasping to self and others, emotions, and habits, then all your stuff floods into your mind, arising vividly and compellingly, making it impossible for what is naturally abiding in your heart to come forth in an authentic way. Everything is the radiance of the essence. Your habitual tendencies and emotions may obscure this truth but with perseverance in the

214

practice, these obscurations will fade. You need to be settled in original heart while gazing for the visions to evolve in an authentic way. Stability will arise naturally as part of the visions, but do not concentrate on returning and remaining while gazing. Concentrate on melting into the vision. At the onset of the visions, acknowledging original heart may not be ongoing, but the visions are one with original heart so merge your open heart with the vision, melting and surrendering into the embrace of the vision, then all obscurations will resolve. The genuine experience of the visions of radiance is a relationship, you are opening yourself to grace.

Unfortunately hindrances and obstacles can arise, which may make gazing impossible for you. Although acknowledging original heart is not intended to be a separate path by itself, you could continue with that practice and as a safeguard keep it within the embrace of the Earth, the sacredness of the vision that is this life, through Earth sitting, Earth walking, and the other suggestions and guidelines we presented in *Part I Earth and Original Heart*. It is a great error to make original heart into a path of mind or a separate practice of its own. Without your heart engaged directly with the balancing force of the visions or the Earth, you can get lost in your mind. If you stay with the practice of original heart without the path of radiance, do it within the way of Earth, and with an intent to

215

complete the four visions in another life. The acknowledgement of original heart without visions of radiance will not bring you to the full resolution of the heart seed and all phenomena.

Pathway of the Outer Fields

The inner fields are the luminous fields of living light in the visions themselves. The outer fields are the supports for their arising: a clear sky, the sun, a candle flame or other light source. You can gaze on the clear blue sky, looking away from the sun on a calm day without any wind. A calm day is important; external wind can stir up your subtle energy, and you want your subtle energy to be very calm and stable. The visions on the sky are subtle, but they allow you to open to the field without squinting, and there is an energetic support, an inner resonance with the openness of the clear sky. If you have access to a private area for gazing on the clear blue sky by all means try it, but you will also need to gaze with a candle or other indoor light source during the times you cannot be outdoors due to wind, clouds, privacy concerns, time of day, and so forth.

If the visions do not arise looking opposite from the sun you can try looking in the direction of the sun, focusing anywhere from the distance of a hand's width to the length of your arm away from the sun free of clouds, but be very, very, careful with your eyes. It is safer for your eyes to look at a sliver of the sun just as it rises or sets on the horizon or at the side of a mountain or a hill. The morning sun at sunrise has a special quality. Not only are the colors particularly beautiful then, but the clarity and freshness of sunrise have an affinity for the quality of the visions. In the early morning and late afternoon, you can gaze on the sun through a screen of trees, or at midday, you can use an open-weave cloth or a woven hat over your eyes to filter the light.

You can also gaze on a reflection of the sun on a slice of polished agate or crystal, or on the surface of still water, all of which can bring out beautiful, clear, strong colors in the vision. When using an agate or crystal sit with your back to the sun and tilt the stone until you get the reflection of the sun. With water, sit facing the water and shield your eyes from the direct rays of the sun coming from above. Some reflections of the sun on water can be hotter and fiercer than others. BE VERY CAREFUL WHEN GAZING ON ANY REFLECTIONS, AND WITH ALL FORMS OF SUN GAZING. SOME PRACTITIONERS HAVE GONE BLIND IN THE PAST. Wear very, very high quality sunglasses that cut 100% of the UV light. This is especially important now with the damage to the upper atmosphere. You do not want to hurt your eyes: they are so crucial for this practice. At night, you can focus directly on the moon. The light from the moon is soothing and cooling to the eyes, especially after sun gazing. Just let the gentle light of the moon flow into your eyes without trying to gaze.

A candle flame that burns brightly without flickering is a safer, reliable, and stable light source. At first, the candle colors may not be as vibrant as sun gazing, but over time the colors will get richer, and the candle is not dependent on weather conditions. The softness of candle light brings out a reciprocal softness in your practice of gazing on many levels. Your breath needs to be very gentle so as not to disturb the flame. That gentleness is reflected in your subtle energy and allows a greater softness and opening in your heart. This is excellent training because even if you can see the visions more easily with a stronger light source, you still need to nurture this quality of gentle openness for the visions to fully mature. Candles vary in quality, in steadiness of flame, and the kind of fumes they emit. Experiment to find a candle that you like. Beeswax candles are very good, also stearin candles, or palm oil candles. Some practitioners prefer a large flame, others a smaller flame. You may also want to experiment with a small flashlight with a single white LED bulb with a cover over it with a pinhole as your light source. DO NOT USE LASER POINTERS, WHICH CAN CAUSE BLINDNESS.

During our retreat, we both started out using sun gazing with sunglasses during the summer months. Once we were fully engaged with the visionary process and the visions were evolving, we stopped using the sun. In addition to the times when the visions arose spontaneously without any external field, for the rest of our retreat, one of us relied mainly on a candle and the other mainly a candle and an LED. Both of us experienced the same progress and ripening of the visions.

The LED is a very stable light source, and it does not flicker or emit fumes. The LED colors are closer to sunlight, more like gazing on the sun's reflection on an agate. There is a quick electric quality to the energy of the LED bulb, but it is not as intense and hot as the sun. You may want to balance it with the gentleness of candle gazing. The brightness of both the sun and the LED is hard on some eyes.

You can also gaze in a darkened room with a slight opening to let light in. The difference between the twilight interior and the ambient brightness outside is often enough to allow the visions to arise. This is not dark retreat, which is a completely different practice. The path of radiance is the path of engaged relationship with living light. The light is your partner and your guide.

It is important to rely on an outer field and practice diligently until the visions arise for you even if you are not focused on the sky, the sun, or a candle or other light source. Of all these fields, rely mainly on the one that suits you, allows your experience of original heart to deepen and the colors of light to arise easily, and brings increase and stability to the visions.

Pathway of the Inner Fields

To bring out the inner fields, there are three gazes, three ways to use your eyes. The first is the gaze associated with the posture of the lion, gazing slightly upward. The second is the gaze associated with the posture of the elephant, keeping both eyes slightly to the side. The third is the gaze associated with the posture of the mountain yogi, keeping your eyes slightly lowered. With any of the three, gaze in an utterly relaxed way without moving your eyes, and try to blink as little as possible. You can encourage moisture in your eyes by squeezing your ear lobes from time to time; there is an energy point there for the eyes. It is important for the practice to not let your eyes dry out. Gaze evenly with both eyes balanced as much as you can.

With any of the outer fields, you need to squint at your light source in order to bring out the visionary field, but you do not want a lot of tension in the muscles around your eyes. Close your eyes gently, just enough to bring out the field of the vision, or close your eyes all the way and then open them slightly until the field of the vision arises. This squinting may feel awkward and difficult to maintain at first, but it is important to the practice. Gradually the field will arise with less and less tension involved. Squinting brings together the outer and inner lights at the opening of the channel of light in each eye and allows the field of the vision to bloom. This does not involve a tunnel focus, it is more of a wide-angle view within the squinting, in much the same way that you use wide-angle vision when blindfolded, which allows you to access the receptive quality of the eyes in a deeper way.

When you squint at any light source, you may at first see rays of light radiating out from the light source. Allow the light ray to come toward your eye. Do not send your eyes toward it, let the squinting bring the light to you, let the light touch your eyes and let the ray unfold into a small field. Rest in original heart and blend with the vision.

In the beginning of your practice, when gazing on a candle flame, LED, or other similar light source you may see a small field of concentric rings and tiny circles centered on the light, which will arise if you are not squinting tightly enough. This is not the visionary field. The small field of rings will remain connected to the physical light and stay centered there. It will not move or evolve.

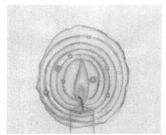

Small veil of rings that is not the field

Close your eyes completely, and then open one eye ever so slightly until the rays of light come out from the light source toward your eye. Keep looking for the field that arises where the inner and outer lights meet; that is where you meet and engage directly with the radiance initiating the visions.

In this practice, you may find yourself confronting your own ideas about meditation depending on your spiritual background. Let go of any ideas or techniques that you may have worked with in the past. This includes working with energy. You should not be doing anything when you gaze except allowing the visions to arise. This is not a meditation. Do not meditate when you gaze. Gaze when you gaze. Rest in original heart and blend, melt, and merge with the visions. Let the light pour into your eyes, let your heart flow into your eyes, let them meet, surrendering to the ineffable grace of their union.

The visionary field begins as a roundish or oval, whitish, very thin, somewhat transparent veil or film that can be flat or billow like a piece of cloth or roll up like a tube of paper. The initial field when unrolled can be very small at first, and depending on your subtle energy, will continue rolling and unrolling until your energies calm down.

When it unrolls, rest your gaze on any circles and spheres in the field and allow the process with the gentle breathing specific to this practice, as you blend and merge softly with the visions. The field will roll up

Genuine visionary field unrolling

again. You have to persevere. Keep your gaze soft with the feeling of the openness of wide-angle vision. You may need to gaze with one eye at a time in the beginning to stabilize the practice. Like waiting for animals, the vision will respond to any tightening of your subtle energy and any grabbing by the mind and roll up again. As you calm down and trust the process unfolding from your heart, the vision will calm down and gazing will calm you further.

The size of the field can appear to be anywhere from a few inches wide to the size of a dinner plate. The inner field or veil of light and all that arises in the visions are a living watery form of radiance, a union of intent on many levels.

You need to have healthy eyes or at the least adequate vision in both eyes. It does not matter if you are nearsighted or farsighted or have perfect vision. Gazing is not just physical sight. It is the union of physical eyes and the primordial visions as seen through the eyes of the heart. The meeting point between outer and inner light is neither inside nor outside but at first you may feel that the visions are very close or "inside" or on the surface of the eye. You may be cross-eyed for a while when you come out of a long gazing session.

The right and left eye have different qualities, in addition to whichever eye you normally favor and other patterns in the way you ordinarily use your eyes. If you cannot use both eyes at once use the eye that is most stable, but keep trying to use the other eye every time you gaze. In general, the right and left eye each have an affinity with a different aspect of the vision. For many practitioners the visionary field from the right eye is more stable at first, but keep checking in on the left eye, it becomes more important later on.

If you are gazing directly off the rays of the sun in the sky or reflected on a polished agate or an LED bulb, you should draw the vision gently off to one side or the other with your eyes; the brightness will not be so intense on your eyes, and the visions will become more stable, which can help them evolve. Even with a candle flame, it is better to look as far away from the light source as you can and still maintain the vision, because looking directly at any light source causes more tension in the muscles around your eyes, and the visions will be jitterier. Drawing the vision to the side is especially important in all forms of sun gazing including using reflections. Some traditions recommend that men draw the visions to the right, women to the left. The subtle energies of men and women are different, and there are many other factors, use the direction that allows the visions to be stable for you.

During all your gazing sessions, sit in one of the postures without moving. Between sessions, keep your movements calm and slow to keep your subtle energies down. Try not to move around very much, and limit or curtail all yogic exercises. Moving slowly and gently between sessions helps keep your subtle energy from being stirred up when you are not gazing.

The best site for sun or sky gazing is on a hill or a mountaintop with an open view of the sky and a view to the east and west that allows you to gaze straight out at the sun's rays in the early morning and late afternoon. However, it is very important that no one see you gazing. Gazing literally opens your heart and as your practice deepens, your heart becomes extremely open. You do not want anyone who is stuck in mind and emotions to get into your eyes and heart at this time. You can absorb their negativity. This can harm your practice and you can develop serious obstacles. When helicopters or even airplanes flew over or near our sun gazing site, we would stop gazing and meditate in a regular cross-legged posture until they passed by. When you choose a site for sun gazing while in retreat, you will need to balance the need for secrecy with the optimal conditions for gazing.

The whole process of the first vision is about bringing all these aspects together with original heart. To allow your heart to open to the visions of radiance, your subtle energy needs to calm down, you need to be in original heart, you need to breathe gently pausing on the out breath, you need to relax without moving in one of the postures, hold your eyes at a certain angle, and squint, all at the same time. Then the luminous visions flow up through the channel of light from your heart to your eyes, then the inner fields bloom from your eyes, then you can begin to engage directly with the intent within the radiance and embark on the last path toward full embrace of essence. Practice day and night and eventually the visions will appear even when you are not using a gazing technique.

Gazing After the Collapse

Today there are many options for the outer fields that were not available in earlier times: different types of candles, white LED bulbs, and machined polished agates, along with high quality sunglasses. But after the collapse when our known world is no more or falling apart, readymade supports for gazing may not be available to you. In this case, you will have to proceed as the peoples of the Earth did, using the sun by day, and in the evening using whatever form of flame you can make with the resources available to you.

In the past, some gazers have constructed small shelters of stone and clay or woven branches and clay for their practice. A *gazing hut* is a small shelter just big enough for one person to sit in with an arm's length space on all sides, and very small holes set in the walls for opening one at a time to let light in at different times of the day and year. We did not use a gazing hut on our retreat, but we did gaze off small cracks of light, and we have built a number of Earth shelters of various kinds, which are relatively easy to build from natural materials depending on where you live with our Mother Earth.

With a gazing hut, you do not need any other light source by day except the ambient brightness of the sky, which allows you to gaze even when there is cloud cover. Gentle on the eyes, the hut provides privacy for

Gazing hut frame

your practice and shelter from the wind. The location of the hut needs to have access to a bright expanse of open sky. Even a forest clearing with an opening toward the sun could work, or on the side of a hill with an opening above the tops of trees. A simple circular hut can be built on a framework similar to that of a small sweat lodge.

Gather an equal number of saplings, eight to twelve, and long enough that when you set them firmly into the ground around the perimeter of your circle they can be bent across the center and overlapped in pairs, creating arches that will allow some extra space above your head when seated. You want to keep the hut small, with the diameter just wide enough that you can lie down.

Set the saplings equally around the circle, making sure you can crawl between the two that will be your doorway. Then bend the saplings opposite one another toward each other and tie them together in arches providing the height for the interior. You may well need to learn how to make cordage or find vines or surface roots of trees in order to lash the saplings together.

Tie smaller branches horizontally around the frame, leaving a low opening to crawl through, adding more and more branches until you have what will look like an upside down basket. Optimally you then plaster the exterior surface with clayish mud mixed with dried grasses or other kinds of fiber, or you can thatch it, which will require gathering a lot more grass. Set small pencil size or smaller sticks through the covering of the hut along the path of the sun, spacing them about a hand's length apart. Place the sticks so they can be removed to allow a small beam of light into the hut as an outer field. For a door, you can hang an opaque cloth or make a framework of lighter branches and thatch it thickly, so that when the door is in place the interior of the hut will be dark enough to gaze on the thin beam of light through one of the pencil size holes. You will have to experiment on where you place the holes, depending on which of the postures you are using and the sun's path across the sky by day and season. You do not need the sun to shine directly through the holes. The difference between the brightness of the day outside, even on all but the cloudiest days, should be enough to gaze on in the darkened interior of the hut. It is always a good idea to camouflage the hut to fit into the local surroundings.

After the collapse, you will need to be very resourceful and creative, and have great perseverance, flexibility, and patience. We cannot emphasize enough how everyone should learn the skills for living with the Earth now, before the collapse.

In the beginning of your practice especially, you may need to work more directly with the sun to engage with the visions, and in addition to reflections of the sun on water, original gazers of the radiance may have also used what are known as *cup and ring* petroglyphs, pecked into large stones in areas that would provide a clear view of the sun and a good safe place to gaze. These circular stone carvings are found throughout the world. Long ago before the fall of humanity into the darkness of the mind, gazers did not have to worry so much about being seen by their own people. Now though, it is vital to be not seen by anyone outside your gazing partners, so you will have to choose your cup and ring site very carefully.

The cup is a shallow bowl shape to hold water, at least one-finger joint's deep so that the water does not evaporate too quickly, and about as wide as your two cupped hands, which will provide enough time for gazing off the reflection of the sun as it tracks across the surface before you have to shift your position.

Shape the cup by using a hammer stone, a stone harder than the cup stone, slowly pecking small chips of stone away.

Cup and ring gazing is similar to gazing with a polished agate, but since the sun's reflection on water is far more intense, be sure to draw the vision to the side and be selective about which reflections you use. This is especially important if you do not have sunglasses. You will have to experiment and be creative with the situations and materials that are available to you. If stones and a suitable site are not available in your area, you can use shells, or a simple wooden bowl can be made by using burning coals to slowly burn a cup shape in a chunk of wood. Carve away the char as the coals cool down and add more coals as necessary, and then burnish the wood with a smooth stone and oil it. By far the safest and most reliable outer field during the day is the gazing hut.

At night, there are a few options to try when candles are no longer available. One is a simple oil lamp, although procuring vegetable oil or animal fat in a wilderness situation requires skill and time, and you may need to eat the fat instead. However, small amounts are not impossible to gather. For a simple lamp, you need a small shallow wooden, clay, or stone bowl with a lip at one end to allow the wick to drape out of the oil. The wick would need to be made by reverse wrapping any good cordage plants that are safe when burned, such as yucca or nettle. The flame may flicker a bit so you will have to experiment with wicks and bowl shapes. Also, try using a woven cover or a flat basket to diffuse the light from a small indoor campfire. Nighttime options will be a lot fewer, and you will need to spend as much of your daylight time gazing as you can.

Gaze especially at sunrise and sundown on the sun through tree branches or right at the edge of the horizon. The quality of light at these times is excellent for gazing, even if for the short amount of time it is available, and there is a special resonance between the early morning light and the visions. Be sure to shield your eyes in some way when gazing with full sunlight during the rest of the day.

The original peoples of the Earth lived naturally as part of the fabric of being. They followed their hearts and knew how and when to seek the sun's help and when not to; they acted with patience and perseverance along a path of return, following a primordial call to oneness. Once the visions begin to ripen you, like others before you, you may be able to gaze directly by the heart light.

A Guide to Radiance

You have experienced original heart blossoming through your heart more and more often, and you know the Earth is your home, now is the time to embark on the path of radiance.

The world is falling into chaos; the world we grew up in is no more. Now as in the times after the collapse, you may not be able to find true guides in human form, but the Earth patiently remains for you offering the way. The Earth and the path of radiance are expressions of the same primordial intent. You are already part of the fabric of being, a member of the Earth's embrace, so the way in, the entrance, the beginning is already all around you in the natural world and in your heart.

Early in the day, before sunrise, in a forested area of good heart where you feel safe and secure, sit on a special spot, one that welcomes you this morning. Sit and remain in original heart for a time, then pray to the holy ones who dwell in the radiance for guidance, sending light from your heart to them throughout space. The holy ones then send rainbow light down to you, pouring down through your crown chakra filling you up with the brilliance of primordial light. Pray to all beings in the area around you, asking for their help and protection, the plants, animals, and insects, the elementals and spirits, asking for their support in entering this path and bringing the four visions of radiance to completion. Quiet yourself, abide in original heart until the sun shines through the trees. Then sit in one of the three gazing postures and look toward the sunlight coming through the trees, close your eyes briefly and slowly open them, just enough to let the rays of the sun come down to blend with your eyes, seeing rainbow colors and circles, sensing the field, feeling the primordial connection. Stay in the posture and gaze with the early morning light.

After the sun has grown too high to gaze comfortably, sit again and abide in original heart in the glow of this primordial light, sense the difference in the tone of your experience of original heart. Pray from your heart, linking your heart with the hearts of the holy ones and the heart of all, forgetting words, experiencing thankfulness directly through the joy and beauty of light. This is the natural, direct way connecting you to the visionary path of radiance.

If you had difficulty seeing the rainbow colors and circles, try again at each sunrise, reconnecting with this prayer of light. Remembering that you are already within the circle where completion is inherent from the beginning, persevere and blend with the blessings of the holy ones.

Heartlamp of Pure Space

As the practice of gazing becomes more natural for you, the essence manifests in your direct perception as luminous colors and shapes of light. Very small circles or spheres coming and going, or vertical or horizontal rays will appear within a field of pure blue light like the sky. If you are gazing on the sky, the field may appear as a glowing blue overlay almost but not quite indistinguishable from the physical blue of the sky. This field of blue and the tiny shapes moving within it are *the heartlamp of pure space.*

How the vision arises for you at this point depends on your subtle energy, channels, and preconceptions, how you habitually use your eyes, the openness of your heart, and so forth. For some practitioners the circles of the *heartlamp of the spheres of light* arise directly when they are introduced to the path, and they do not see the blue field.

Heartlamp of the Spheres of Light

You begin to see slightly larger circles glowing with an inner light like cells under a microscope, some as if drawn or lightly shaded with a pencil, others with rainbow color rims. This is *the heartlamp of the spheres of light*. You may perceive one or two coming and going, possibly even a river of circles or spheres. But eventually one circle or sphere will settle into your field and remain: this is a special aspect of your heart seed.

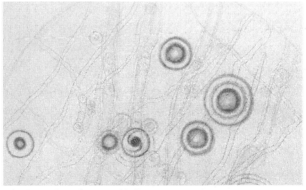

Circles and continuum of light

You will also see long strands of smaller luminous circles like strings of pearls or rosaries of light sweeping through the field with a fluid motion. At times there may be other smaller circles attached to them. All strands together are the *continuum of light*, the initiatory energy within the radiance of the essence, a continuity of intent that pervades all manifestation. From the strands of light in the visions to the DNA in our cells, the same continuum of intent permeates and guides our every experience at all levels.

This continuity arises moment by moment in the world, in your life, and in the process of gazing. It can arise as habitual tendencies, obscurations, and rampant emotions, or as acknowledgement of original heart and the continuum of light. All structures are maintained by holding to their apparent reappearance moment by moment in seemingly coherent order, over and over. The intent of the essence manifests continuity to teach and guide, providing an environment for change that includes a sense of a basic stability in the world as a foundation for learning and growing. Sky above, Earth below, cycles of seasons, and night and day express a fundamental functional kindness as a context for our choices, a sacred continuity of intent outside personal identity, a continuity always offering a way home, a way to return to origin for every being, and this continuity manifests directly in the visions as the continuum of light.

You do not follow the strands as they move through the field instead allow the continuum of light to approach and come to rest on any stable circles of light that have settled in your field. Gaze without wavering, without holding, without trying to manipulate the vision in any way. As you enter the visions, the movements of the continuum will mirror the turbulence of your mind. Let go and let your energies subside and the strands will eventually come to rest. They are powerful teachers. They are a particular activating form of the intent of essence guiding you to fruition.

Heartlamp of Original Heart

The heartlamp of original heart sees and acknowledges the visions as direct displays of the sacred intent woven throughout the fabric of being, the radiance of essence. The essence is the source, the primordial potential. All the other heartlamps and aspects of the path are not separate from the essence in any way. Therefore, it is essential to settle in original heart recognizing the essence in the display as a blended acknowledgement. This is the catalyst that allows the visions to unfold in an authentic sequence and for all aspects of the senses and mind to be purified.

Too often when people embedded in the cultures of mind receive these teachings, they think their experience of original heart and the radiance and fail in their attempt in the visionary path of radiance. You must be honest and humble in your assessment of your spiritual practice. It is vital for your practice to be in original heart while you gaze: without true acknowledgement of original heart, the visions will not arise and mature in an authentic natural way free of the distortions of mind. Now, as well as in the chaos of the coming age, you can always rely on the Earth to help you to a genuine experience of original heart, with or without a human guide.

As you gaze in original heart, you blend with the effulgent potential within the visions, and the natural attribute of the essence that is a unity beyond union and separation unfolds from the heart seed, spontaneously present, an indwelling purity that permeates all beings limitless as space.

Four Actions

As you become more and more embraced within the visions, you gradually let go of all that hinders or obstructs the growth of your heart seed. And as those obscurations fade, there is a corresponding development, an acknowledgement of an unclouded perception, slowly letting go of all concepts, thoughts, and emotions, approaching, revealing, realizing the truth just as it is, and then finally only essence. The four visions are a gradual process that cannot be rushed. The timing of your development is different for each practitioner, but in addition to the basic instructions, there are some general guidelines for each stage of the path.

Seven actions are sometimes presented as aids to practice on any path. They represent ways to focus your subtle energy so you do not spin out and create hindrances for your practice. They keep you centered appropriately at each phase of the practice. At first they are guidelines you aspire to, and gradually they become your way of being at each stage.

The first level is the *action of a bee*. Like a bee gathering nectar and returning to the hive, blended with the Earth, guided by the pulse of our Mother, you have certainty of your direction. On the path of primordial grace, this means you acknowledge original heart in your direct experience and trust that all that naturally arises is sacred and consecrated as an expression of the intent of essence.

The second level is the *action of a swallow*. Swallows are extremely diligent. Once you have complete confidence in the visionary path of radiance, with no doubts that all obscurations, emotions, and habitual tendencies will be purified through this path, and you know in your heart that you can reach fruition in this lifetime, put the teachings into practice in full time retreat. Like a swallow building its nest, focus entirely on the practice.

The third level is the *action of a wounded deer*. Stay in solitude, in complete retreat far from people immersed in the cultures of mind, and give up all distractions of the mind that you may still harbor in yourself.

The fourth level is the *action of a mute*. Do not speak, remain in silence.

In the visionary path of radiance, the next three levels on the traditional list are not entered into as actions but arise naturally through your engagement with the visions, and their qualities are reflected in aspects of the signs for the second and third visions.

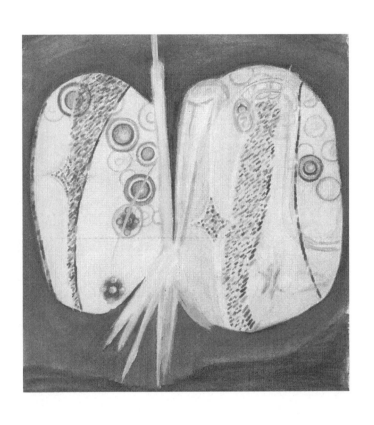

The Cycle of the Four Visions

The four great visions of radiance are part of an organic living process, a natural cycle, and within that cycle, there are whole arenas of experience, each with their own texture of transformation. There are landmarks on the path, gateways through which you enter another stage of the visionary process, and the stages of this path are spoken of as the four visions, but they are more clearly understood as four aspects of a single visionary process that is moving you toward the indivisible oneness of return to essence. The four visions are not separate events, or snapshots that slowly come into focus: they are a living visionary process that extends over a period of years of day and night practice. The cycle of the visions can be divided like a circle into four segments, four aspects of experience similar to the cycle of the seasons and the stages of growth in a plant or a human, but they are still part of a single circle of experience.

On this primordial path, you surrender to the original heart, settle your body and eyes in specific postures and gazes, and breathe in a specific way, to open a very subtle channel that leads from your heart to your eyes. Nourished by the soil of your heart that you have prepared by all the previous practices, the luminous seed in your heart opens and begins to grow upward toward your eyes, giving rise to the fluid, ongoing experience called the four visions. Following the stages of the growth of a plant, the seedling of light emerges and puts out seed leaves as the onset of the first vision, and you perceive the radiance directly as it truly is. The seedling grows, puts out more leaves and the first buds of flowers as you become part of the increasing experiences of the second vision, and then matures and blossoms as the total effulgence of the third vision. The energy then turns inward, concentrating the dynamic force of the essence to set seed in the fourth vision, which brings you to the ultimate resolution of all phenomena, all radiance as a seamless whole.

The primary language of this cycle is visual, the intent of essence communicating directly with you outside of words, engaging and ripening you, through a corresponding ripening of the shapes and colors of living light in the visions transforming your very being. This visionary process is marked by extraordinary beauty. We are both artists, and we kept sketchbooks of the visions as they unfolded during our retreat. Since color is such an integral aspect of the visions, we have included only a few black and white images here. As a companion text to this chapter, we recommend our book *Luminous Heart of Inner Radiance: Drawings of the Tögal Visions*, with numerous color illustrations from our sketchbooks.

The First Vision

Direct Perception of the Nature of Radiance

As the circles and spheres of light become more stable in your experience, you will start to notice that one or two circles are becoming familiar. They appear whenever you gaze, and they begin to feel like old friends. The continuum of light will start coming around these circles. At first the strands will be moving fast, like hawks diving and swooping away, then slower and closer, passing by with the gravity and dignity of large animals, and finally, hovering over the circles like bees approaching a flower. When you perceive three or more circles or spheres that are stable in close arrangement next to each other, and the rosaries of light slow down and abide within these circles to a slight degree, this is the beginning of the first vision of this path, *direct perception of the nature of radiance*. You are perceiving the radiance of the essence just as it is, unadorned, unconfused, beyond all speculation, concepts, and symbols.

There are specific signs that arise naturally through your practice. They are not actions that you engage in; they arise within and through you, as the practice ripens you. In the first vision, *you are like a tortoise placed in a bowl*. You do not want to move from the postures;

you do not want to stop practicing, and you have no interest in other activities. *You are like a mute.* You do not want to talk. *Your mind fades like frost in the morning sun.* At times, your acknowledgement of original heart spontaneously blossoms into inner radiance, embracing your thoughts as they arise; you have no interest in following them.

Throughout the first vision, what you are seeing is not as important as how your mind is changing, becoming more and more willing to surrender to the heart, more willing to allow the heart to open. As the circles stabilize and the strands of the continuum of light slow down, they are reflections of your energies becoming more refined, and inner radiance blooms in and of itself more frequently. Your obscurations are being purified, and your heart has opened, but you have not yet come into the full scope of its potential. If you were to die at this stage of the practice, you would be reborn in a life and situation that would allow you to continue this path.

From the beginning of your practice, it is important to be able to distinguish between expressions of prana and the genuine visions. Prana forms are manifestations of the mind and subtle energy. These projections are crystalline, detailed, edgy and electric, and at times almost photographic. They flash on quickly as images that are recognizable and understandable to the intellect, and depending on your background they can include images from spiritual belief systems. The authentic visions of radiance are organic, fluid, and cellular. They have a softer elemental feeling accompanied by a sense of awe or open wonder and joy at the approach of an unknowable yet strangely familiar presence. If you see deities and elaborate symbolic shapes early in the visions, they are prana, do not dwell on them, just let them go as you would any other thought, and blend in original heart with the circles and spheres and the continuum of light.

The visual field of the genuine vision has a number of transparent or translucent layers, roundish or oval veils, usually hazy, white or gray, glowing with a soft light, often billowing or rolling and unrolling like a luminous map until your subtle energies begin to slow down. The *pencil field* is the closer layer that you meet first. The continuum of light and most of the circles that arise within this field have grey outlines as if drawn in pencil. Some of the circles may have rainbow rims, although in general they will not have the vivid colors of the following visions.

Whatever arises in the vision, blend with it, but do not hold to any of it. Allow the visions to arise naturally. When the authentic visions arise as rainbow color light, concentric circles, diamonds, clusters of drops, coils of joy, or shapes that look like simple flowers, rest your gaze on them. Do not get lured into following after them. The circles themselves can be very compelling; there is a calming, centering, almost mesmerizing quality to their roundness. The continuum of light will appear more restless, wilder and unpredictable or gliding by, flowing as if pulled by a tidal force, but they are showing you the restless force of your subtle energy that you gradually tame by the whole process of gazing. For the visionary process to ripen in an authentic way, gaze in open original heart. The most important aspect of the first vision is that original heart is becoming a deeper more fluid blended experience. There is less separation, divisions are falling away. When you stop gazing at the end of a session, you notice that what was once a subtle experience now has a depth to it, and more stability.

Some traditions teach that the lion posture strengthens your connection with the continuum of light, the elephant posture with the circles, and the mountain yogi posture with original heart. In the beginning when you are stabilizing the field you may find that you are favoring the right eye. Your right eye has an affinity with the circles and spheres, which are naturally calmer and calming. The left eye has an affinity for the continuum of light and even though the strands are more active at first, they play a key role in the development of the entire visionary process, so do not neglect the left eye.

Do not speculate about the visions while you are gazing. Do not indulge in thinking about how they arise, counting, measuring your progress, worrying, wondering if you are doing it right. Go directly to your heart and the visions. The path of radiance is the path of no doubts, the path of direct experience. Give yourself to the visions. It is very important to remember that you are not making the visions happen. You are not visualizing or manipulating them. You are allowing, surrendering, entering into a profound relationship, a sacred dimension with no outside, no inside, no self and other, ideally a tender gentle embrace. However, stuff comes up, your mind can churn; just ride it out, all the anguish and the insights, let them go. The vision will calm down, and one day you will not care as much about the doings of your mind. You will give up your fascination with the astonishing at times claustrophobic variety of your thoughts and perceptions, and give yourself utterly to the visions. As you experience original heart naturally becoming more and more stable, you gain confidence that the practice is carrying you to fruition. A great joy arises. This is not bliss; this is the first landmark, the joy of letting go and allowing your open luminous heart to blend with the circles and the continuum of light, merging with the visions of radiance, entering the great primordial joy returning you to origin.

The visions are organic, and each vision evolves naturally into the next one. In the beginning especially, each practitioner will have different experiences of the stages of metamorphosis that you undergo as the visions move you toward resolution, but there are specific qualities to the visions and definite signs that must arise at each stage, landmarks providing a guide on this crucial journey.

There are a number of ways to distinguish between the first and second vision. Some traditions emphasize increasing size of the circles and the field of the vision. Others emphasize more color or the ripening of original heart as guidelines. There is a fluidity to the process. Your experience of original heart and the visions evolve together, but as they evolve, your experience can be like a wave, touching upon new aspects of the vision and deepening qualities of your open heart then falling back, not too far, more like a gentle incoming tide, slowly, steadily lapping farther up the shore.

The Second Vision

Becoming Radiance

As the visions of radiance continue to evolve, you enter the second vision, *becoming radiance*. The visual field, the circles, and the continuum of light become larger, and the rainbow colors begin to stabilize. You begin to see more of the basic fundamental shapes of light: concentric circles, coils of joy, diamonds, clusters of spheres, stripes, spokes, lattices, multicolored shimmering fields, cruciform flower shapes, and so forth. These forms are simple, organic, and natural. They are not symbolic, they are expressions of living light. Your direct perception of them may be affected by your cultural conditioning; someone with a long background in visualization practices could see these forms of light assimilated to the perspective of their beliefs. Again, be careful to distinguish between prana and the visions. The basic shapes in their pure elemental presence have a power just as they are, that both validates and goes beyond religious structures.

As the pencil field becomes more and more transparent, you see one or more layers of color fields, often very molten and active at first, with patterns of rainbow colors or fields of varied colors, or a turbulent surging flood of colored circles rushing across and filling the field.

The circles and the continuum of light increase in size and number. They have a more tangible presence as they evolve, and their colors increase in intensity. The size of the elements of the visions will be seen in relation to whatever outer field you are gazing on. If you are gazing on the sky, your larger concentric circles may seem the size of mountains and valleys. If you are indoors you see them in proportion to cups, bowls, tables, windows, or doors, but all comparisons of size as well as sense of depth become more fluid as part of the increase.

The visions are neither inside or outside, but you begin to experience a spatial shift in how you perceive the visions. You may feel like you are entering them, or you may feel a sudden vast expanse within the field of the vision as if you are looking from a high mountain top although the circles and the continuum of light are the same size they were a moment before. Your mind is letting go of ordinary parameters of size, dimension, and perspective. The brain's contribution to what you see is fading away, and you are seeing more purely what the retina is seeing through the eyes of the heart. This is *breaking the seal*.

As the visions of radiance increase, original heart becomes stable; your experience of the vision and your experience of original heart are joined. You come to a realization that inner radiance is looking through its own eyes, recognizing, merging with inner radiance of all manifestation. This blending is a pivotal time in the visions and is called *crossing the pass*. Now that you are becoming the visions, the visions themselves become the true sign of your progress on the path.

Wisdom stars appear, curvilinear diamond shapes woven of impossibly fine fibers of light. They can appear suddenly, coming and going with a movement and a quality very much like hummingbirds. They are a pure expression of grace appearing within the visions. As they increase in number and in the complexity of their forms, bands of flickering rainbow lights that change in specific complex patterns appear within them.

The simple cruciform flower shapes begin to mature into displays of clearly distinguishable seed mandalas of tranquil and dynamic energies based on a core arrangement of four circles of light around a central circle. The *tranquil seed mandalas* can be of various combinations of colors. They may have a single rainbow rim or many rims like ripples on a still pond. They reflect the calm centered energy of potential in equilibrium, and they sometimes appear as an equal cross. The *dynamic seed mandalas* are based on the same core arrangement and are much more dynamic, almost explosive, with colored circular shapes and bands coming off the four compass points and the diagonals. They are an expression of initiating forceful energies and their presence has a feeling of movement even when they are stationary. As the tranquil and dynamic seed mandalas increase in number, they also become more complex and differentiated in color and shape.

Around this time, you should focus your attention on the left eye. Not only have the circles grown in size but one strand of the continuum of light will have grown larger and denser. This strand is ripening, and soon a deity, a single unadorned bodily form, will begin to manifest. The deity arises out of a ripening strand of light that may or may not be the same strand associated with the three circles of the first vision. Within the continuum of light, the deity appears at first as a simple circle head with a crown protuberance, then the upper body, then a complete bodily form, and then many bodily forms. This is a reflection of the natural evolution of the essence within you as your confusion and obscurations continue to fade. The deity or divine being is your heart seed, your very being maturing and developing into a bud of truth. It is a major expression and sign.

In the second vision, you are like *a person in the throes of a serious illness.* You lose your sense of vanity or shame about your body. Your speech is like that of *a divine fool.* Your words flow directly from your heart unfettered by cultural constraints. The linear coherence of your thoughts and words is breaking down; your words can arise spontaneously from another dimension of experience. You are like *a person under the influence of a sacred mind-altering plant.* Your ordinary thinking has dissolved into original heart and your perceptions are less afflicted by concepts. The confusion of fixating on the apparent solidity of the manifest world is receding. Holding to attachments or hostilities vanishes. The veils that keep you from perceiving purely from the heart, the veils that keep you from merging with the oneness of all manifestation, are going away. You are moving beyond concepts of likes and dislikes, beyond accepting and rejecting. You do not care what you are wearing or not wearing; it helps to be in retreat. You still take care of your health but you are completely immersed in the visions, you give up all caring about any aspect of the body that does not support or is not actually involved in gazing. The traditional metaphors for the signs at this stage are expressions of a shifting in your experience that can feel like an altered state. The structures that hold concepts together, the cultural glues, are dissolving. You have not yet reached the place where it seems normal to be so fluid, and the unfamiliar feels extraordinary.

The bud of the heart seed is beginning to open. If you die at this time, you will recognize and merge directly with the radiance of the essence as it appears after death, either as the openness of a clear blue autumn sky or as the visions of radiance, which may arise for you then in a particularly vivid and unobstructed way.

As the visions continue to evolve, you begin to see larger colored circles coming together, joining, blending with one another. These rainbow colored circles of light in union are expressions of the continuing ripening of the vision and your heart seed. At first, you will perceive the *unions* as circles of rainbow light coming together like two lovers in an embrace, and eventually some will develop halos, auras, and bodily forms. In some traditions, unions are part of the third vision, but circle unions begin to arise long before they mature within the effulgence of the third vision.

The threshold between the second and the third vision is just as fluid as the transitions between the other visions. There are not really four visions: they are part of a seamless organic whole. To divide the process into four stages is a way of organizing the various aspects of visionary experience and transformation that you come to in the practice, but do not be caught up in measuring your progress.

The Third Vision

Effulgence of Radiance

The visionary field grows larger, and there is an even more molten, alive, visceral quality to the visions and the way they arise. This is the onset of the third vision, *effulgence of radiance*. The visceral totality of all your experience and the arising of the mandalas in the visions characterize the third vision. The seedling of light matures, blossoms, and then blooms more and more effulgently, abundantly, beyond measure, and the displays of the vision become all-encompassing. Inner radiance expands outward to the fullest extent and shines on all levels of the visions and ordinary experience.

The simple forms of the holy ones that began to appear in the color fields around the same time as the deity now begin to mature. As they come and go within the color fields, they gradually become more complex in their forms; the single spheres with halos and elongated cocoon-like bodies of light develop as single figures and also within the embrace of union.

The arising of the deity in the second vision is an expression of the sky-like openness of your heart blossoming into inner radiance, recognizing itself through you. The holy ones that are maturing within the third vision are expressions of the larger aware knowingless knowing, the intent of the essence outside personal manifestation, the luminous net of compassionate intent that weaves the entire world vision we find ourselves within. The holy ones are reflections of the spontaneously arising nature of essence within which the spheres of individual awareness learn, grow, and ripen.

The unions continue to appear as single unions, then in groups, and finally in patterns of groups of unions, forming nets, necklaces, webs of living light, and vast towering three-dimensional forms of light weaving countless worlds of intent. The displays extend beyond the light source, moving beyond the supports as they evolve into full-blown *mandalas* in an organic, molten, soft, upwelling of the uttermost depths. The mandalas are organic, rhythmic arrangements that bloom around or are associated with the forms of the holy ones. They will begin to hold steady and some may abide for long periods of time floating within an oceanic depth. Whole fields of luminous nets appear with tranquil or dynamic seed mandalas at every intersection, and energy masses of tiny lights of tiny bodily forms, and all the while the fabric of the familiar world is literally pulling apart, unraveling into companion lights.

The world of your external experience continues to soften. What was once a solid, fixed reality becomes less and less held in place by concepts of time and space. Substance is perceived as it actually is, living light, the radiance of essence, and the landscape or your body may suddenly burst into rays of pure colored light. You begin to see countless holy forms and holy realms pervading all of space yet resting upon your finger. Whole universes suddenly unfold from the vaporous shell of perceptions that a moment before had been an elbow or a hand.

If you are not already gazing on the dark within the light of the visions themselves, at the edge of sleep, pay attention to that threshold now. Another kind of seeing awakens, the eyes seeing directly by the glow of the heart light.

In the third vision, you are like *an elephant in a mud hole*. There is a visceral, molten quality to the visions and all your experience, a viscous fluid density, a weight and a freedom at the same time, as you gaze and as you walk around. It is an experience of being totally immersed, totally engaged in the tactile, transitory quality of experience and yet not caught in any way. All details of your experience are more vivid, more densely textured, and more fleeting, all at the same time. There is a totally blossoming effulgent quality to all your experience, and yet you are coming closer and closer to the essence. Habitual tendencies, emotional patterns, concepts of time and space are falling away; the elephant is just about to come out of the mud.

Your speech is like that of *an elemental water spirit that sings with a particularly beautiful voice*. Through the ripening of the wisdom of oneness, the archaic and primordial rhythms of the union of heaven and Earth permeate every word spoken or heard. Your thoughts can arise in meter and rhyme. You can hear and sing songs that you have never heard, or familiar songs, all evoking celestial sound emerging from and returning to light.

Your mind is like *a person who has recovered from a disease and is now immune.* You have no fear of being caught again in the confined shell of separation. You are outside all obscurations of the mind, with no fear of catching ignorance again. You cannot go back. All your philosophical systems fall away, and there arises a direct seamless knowing. All the structures of belief that have supported your path this far are empty shells on the shore of a vast ocean of this knowing. You feel a kind of nostalgia without longing welling up from your heart, a tenderness as the manifest world is turning to light and you are moving away from solidity, moving closer and closer to the essence.

The whole expanse of the third vision is beyond measure, but as expansive and all-encompassing as this experience is, it is still not the complete return to origin: you are still within the realm of radiance, the realm of manifestation. As the vision evolves to the fullest extent, lines of light will pour from clusters of tranquil seed mandalas and holy ones to connect with your heart center. If you die at this point you will be taken into the filaments of light and drawn into the heart centers of those expressions of the inner radiance, or those forms of light may be drawn into your heart center. Either way, through that transference, you merge with the essence and disperse into the light mass of inner radiance.

The Fourth Vision

Resolution of Radiance

The appearance of the filaments of light is a sign of the beginning of the fourth vision, *resolution of radiance*. The fine lines of light that connect with your heart center from the clusters of tranquil seed mandalas and the holy ones as the effulgence crests at the furthest reaches of expansion are not only visual, they are felt within all that is left to resolve. The experience is that of very fine fibers of light weaving a brilliance out of whatever is left of you, taking the leftovers of your beingness and changing them into the brilliance of manifesting light. Through the complete path of the four visions, the radiance of the essence and the rosaries of light that are the nucleus or germ of the heart seed are fully matured, and then all manifestation dissolves into the essence. Whatever is left of the perceptions and appearances maintained by the deepest roots of single identity fall away. The continuity of all experience literally ceases. There is a break, a gap, nothing not nothing. This is the culmination, the resolution of all phenomena gathered together as a seamless whole.

The process of the fourth vision is very similar to the way a plant goes to seed. The plant no longer puts out buds and the final delicate flower petals dry into shapes of darkening and opaque color. All the energy of the plant goes toward the seed. With the same inexorable power that drove their increase, slowly, unerringly, the visions recede from the limitless horizons of the full expanse of the third vision. The rhythms of expansion are changing; the visions are beginning the great inward turning that leads to the resolution of radiance. The energy that drives the effulgence of the third vision, ever expanding, molten, and fluid, begins to fold inward like a wave cresting and rolling back into itself, concentrating the full force of the effulgence into the seeds of oneness. The generative energy of pure potential is shifting from outward expansion to focusing that energy into the awakened seeds.

This coalescing movement, the tidal pull of inward turning, first arises as fruit and pod-like mandalas of the seeds of oneness and the clusters with the filaments of light, and finally in nebulas of countless tranquil seed mandalas at the furthest reaches beyond time and space, galaxies of oneness, appearing as interstellar clouds emanating out of unimaginable blue-black depths, reflecting the brilliance of the implosion and expansion at the edge of the essence itself.

Waves of clusters, galaxies of oneness, unions, and single forms wash through the field of the vision, gradually fewer and fewer. Total effulgence is ebbing, a quality in the visions like the downward pull of energy within a plant or tree in autumn. There is a quietness, an inward turning, light returning to the heart. This is the most profound of all the visions. There is a compelling quality for the last vestiges of manifest identity in riding the visions outward, surrendering to the glory and the wonder of ever increasing experience, like a waxing moon reaching an effulgence without limit, the mountaintop beyond all mountaintops, the sky beyond all sky. But having embraced the full scope of all experience, as the visions turn that vastness inward, condensing it into the now awakened seed, the last bit of identity still residing in the body rides the vision inward and downward in the last surrendering, surrendering even the expanse of the radiance.

A single circle appears in the midst of the condensing vision. It may be the same familiar circle as in the first vision or it may be a new one, and it becomes your guide. All your experience is now seamless. Simple gestures of nature, the colors of autumn leaves, dew drops on a blade of grass, an apple by candlelight, are no more or less amazing than the visions or the bursts of light. There is a complete acceptance of all levels of experience as a unity forever beyond sundering, and with this unity comes a softness and a depth like the endless bottom of the sea, a massive oceanic tenderness, relentless, fluid, and immense. The four great qualities, openness, transcendence, oneness, and spontaneous presence are all one now, they are the same, no longer divisible into four, the perfection of the single sphere.

During the fourth vision, you are like *a rainbow in a mist*. This is literal. Perceptions that hold your body together are melting away. Like a mist in the midday sun, effortlessly, naturally, you are dissolving into light. *Speech is like an echo*. Even when you hear your own voice, it feels as if no one is speaking. Your voice is turning to a mist as well; it is not separate from the textures of other sounds. Words have no power to hold anything. You experience only *thoughts that flash like lightning*, and they fall away as soon as they arise. You are like *a person hit in the heart by an arrow*. The resolution of radiance happens suddenly, all experience exhausted in an instant; there is no way to avoid returning to the essence, there is no one there to stop it.

The field of the vision grows smaller, and you may see oval openings in the field, *black holes*, like oil on water, but with a very different quality. They are not floating on a surface, they are the depth of the essence showing through, hovering at the edge of perception. You literally recapitulate the path; layers of veils of all the visions return, and the pencil field map from the first vision becomes more apparent again. Suddenly, there is a feeling, a wave deep within your whole being, a wave of all space and then, hitting the bottom of all experience, resolving and becoming essence, nothing not nothing, no perceiver and nothing to perceive, yet you re-manifest with a memory beyond memory.

From within the resolution of essence as essence, there is no one there, no one to decide, but the totality of your aspirations and intent all along the path will propel you to remain in the full embrace of primordial being, the depths of origin, or re-manifest into the radiance of this world transformed, abiding in the natural state of original being in this lifetime.

The Return

Outside of words, a depth beyond any kind of depth, no mind or body or world. Like a single low tone from a timpani drum. Time has dissolved, with space and words no more, beyond timelessness, nothing not nothing.

Then the return, as if one whole being, all of experience, begins to pulsate with blood again, suddenly, seamlessly, reappearing, remanifesting, nothing came back, and yet a primordial memory held in every cell, a blue-black known with an intent both personal and outside of being, inexpressible yet its return is all appearances.

We walk outside in the bright spring air, talking quietly with each other. We talk as before of experience, though our eyes look now through this depth and see only its reflection. Everything is the vision, an experience so deep and unassailable, your bones know it, your eyes know it, your heart knows it, your hair, nothing that is not now suspended in a vast tenderness beyond all knowing. We are no more, yet we perceive and function as an essence embraced. All words, all thoughts are bright bubbles, bits of foam, floating on the surface of immeasurable radiant depths.

As you reach the feeling we call the wave you arrive at the very edge of the essence, yet still a net of identity holds the last trace of a you in place until it too pops, and then all phenomena, all perception, and your body dissolve away to pure essence, beyond oneness. You return to the same body yet different, the same character yet changed, the same world yet you see through everything. You return with the essence known. There are no boundaries to this knowing, no barriers of time or space. You are the clear essence, the heart of all, deep, centerless, aware, a humble seed manifesting in apparent form only to benefit.

When you return you take on the semblance of a life again; you may appear to have ordinary hopes and fears. You may seem charismatic and bold, or quiet and plain. To meet the realm of choice from within oneness is to be a rainmaker who brings the long-sought rain simply by being who you are, nothing not nothing, inseparable with everything. You are a field of natural emanation to comfort, counsel, protect, or teach. You appear with an intent that is visible or invisible depending upon the perceiver. This spontaneous, effortless, selfless way is how emanations arise, naturally, fluidly, out of the pure shell of your return, your sphere of essence. You have become one with the corona of the essence, the nature of all the holy ones.

Landmarks on the Path

A summary of the way your experience of the practice will arise for you as each of the four visionary stages ripen.

When you have experienced the coming together of the acknowledgement of original heart and the visionary practice of radiance, and feel within your heart the wondrous warmth of a great joy as you realize that this path will carry you to origin in this life, you will have reached the first landmark, the *joyous*.

When you have recognized as you gaze that the visions are not in the candle flame or in the sky, but are pouring outward through your eyes, you will have reached the second landmark, *clearing eyes*.

When you have perceived three stable circles and the continuum of light coming together as you grow more and more one with the display, you will have reached the third landmark, the *kindled heart*.

When you have experienced an increase in the display and have recognized that inner radiance is looking through its own eyes, you have reached the fourth landmark, *crossing the pass*.

When you have perceived the bodily form of the single deity, and have experienced the purification of all that held you from recognizing that the deity is you, you will have reached the fifth landmark, *touching purity*.

When you have perceived the color displays and the tranquil and dynamic seed mandalas purely from your heart, just as they are, you will have reached the sixth landmark, *seeing clearly*.

When you have perceived the primordial mothers and fathers of light in union as separation falls away and you see that there is no way to be separate, you will have reached the seventh landmark, *reaching union*.

When you have perceived clusters with filaments of light connecting with your heart as all conceptual thoughts holding time and space fall away, you will have reached the eighth landmark, *becoming light*.

When you have perceived the ripening of the mandalas and the galaxies of oneness, you will have reached the ninth landmark, the *threshold of oneness*.

When you have come to the heart of the inwardly directed ocean-like depth of the single sphere and all radiance including that depth resolves into essence, you will have reached the tenth landmark, *becoming essence*.

A Seed for a New Beginning

Given the level of human insanity today, it may be increasingly difficult to believe or envision that some humans could live after the coming collapse and return to the sacred circle of life. In our hearts, we see a future where small groups of people come back to a life lived with our First Mother in original heart and begin the long journey of healing.

The circle of life holds a seed for a new beginning. In that seed are groups of Earth people who are spiritually responsible for themselves, spheres of influence responding to other spheres like concentric circles forming on a pond in a light rain. They are individual, humble, and aware, offering whatever they can to the group and are given whatever they need, always balanced in union within the whole. Each group is a small circle of people knitted together, a flock of birds moving as one through their hearts, a living consensus moving within the flow of original heart. No separation, no lesser or higher, a call and response in the moment wedded to all the other calls.

Do you see yourself in such a seed? Do you see that you can return to origin? Can you see yourself leaving the structures of the mind and living with the openness of the heart? Can you envision yourself bringing your wants and needs down to virtually nothing to open to a life filled to overflowing?

Our world vision we call Earth can be lived in simplicity, within the wonder and living glory that naturally arises. You can still learn how to do this, the techniques are few, but the most important is an open aware heart. Knowing how to live with our Earth is crucial to shed the basis of the fear underlying contemporary culture. To know in your heart that wherever you are you can build a shelter, find water, build a fire, and find food liberates you from the terrible curse of the fall, the fear of being helpless, the fear of being lost. We are here to live simply within this vision of the natural world, without the fears and burdens of separation, following the personal signs and messages in a heart to heart union with the divine, a spiritual life played out through countless lives embraced by this flow of intent.

But here we are now on an endangered planet, and human insanity is reaching suicidal proportions. Species extinction is pandemic. The great diversity of natural life is vanishing due to our actions. The ignorance of man is cresting, soon to turn inward and crash down upon itself, an unfortunate reflection of the natural cycle of decline ending this time in unnecessary tragedy. This is almost too bleak to comprehend, yet this is also a time of setting seed, a time of turning inward toward origin, toward what is essential. This is a time to set the seed of your spiritual journey, to concentrate and focus your life, your intent, and all your love into a form that can engender new life. You can embrace this time and change within it, or you can hold to what is collapsing and deny the reality of our situation or try to wish it away.

During times of decline and dissolution there is a gap, an opening where you can choose to shift your perspective and change. Within this gap, this extraordinary space in time, you can set the seed of new aspects of your path and change within it.

The path of the primordial grace will help you to learn the ways of the Earth, and to breath in rhythm with our First Mother, to become a blended individual, one within a wholeness, with a sky-like heart moving within the circle of intent of all life. This book is a seed and if sprouting on fertile soil it will guide you to look with open eyes to perceive this world from your heart, open like the sky, and with a view unclouded by the mind you will know what to do with this opening within the collapse. Setting seed and an open heart are intertwined with a purpose that all life prospers, experiencing and learning within the active movement of a generative love. If you come from an open heart relating with all that naturally manifests, you will experience this love. It is this generative love that will heal the wounds of our world, preparing the ground for another age.

We each have an opportunity and a sacred responsibility now at the time of setting seed to make choices that will engender a future of harmony within the radiance of essence arising naturally all around us. We pray that out of the dissolution of this age will come another age when the natural world will be seen again through the heart, as the heart. There will be no separation, no distinction of other, but a knowing loving embrace of a sacred vision, like the curving petals of a flower unfolding and radiating outward from the seed, a natural blending of union, fluid like water, expansive like the air, brilliant like the sun.

Glossary

A summary of some key words used in the text.

Embrace An experience of total and complete resolution of all being, both physical and spiritual, your sphere of influence blended effortlessly into the essence, like water into water, a seamless oneness. The resolution of the visionary path of radiance. See *Return*.

Essence Origin, the primordial essence beyond all aspects of this world, beyond all beliefs, all concepts, all perspectives, and all experience, a luminous knowingless knowing that cannot be defined, a primordial purity of intent that is beyond emptiness and spacious beyond all concepts of space, absolute potential, neither tangible nor intangible, yet its expression is everywhere.

Heart   The indwelling heritage of natural connection with the heart of all being. The natural seat of human knowing, our true center of gravity outside cultural parameters and ordinary perceptions. The doorway to a fluid grounded knowingless knowing that is engaged rather than separate, a natural responsiveness, a way of knowing and caring that joins us with all life. A view that cannot be nailed down or defined in specific terms and can only be felt and experienced in an allowing way.

Heart Seed   The luminous seed of oneness abiding in your heart activated through the visionary path of radiance. Seat of the primordial visions of radiance, a fluidity beyond coming or going, beyond time and space, an endless ocean already present within you out of which the manifest forms of living light reflect from within your heart. The essence abiding within your heart as the luminous manifestations of holy forms.

Inner Radiance   A deeper experience of the natural luminosity of original heart, the intent of the essence blossoming, opening beyond thought or description, fluid, molten, luminous joy, evanescent yet palpable, arising as anything and everything, from the shining dewdrop on a leaf in the early morning to the light of your own heart. A heightened experience of original heart spreading out of your heart like light across the sky with an innocent joy.

Original Heart   The true sky of your heart, an embrace of all being, an openness, natural, and abiding. An expansive sense of knowing outside all conceptualization, an openness that has no boundaries, edges, or restrictions of any kind. A tone of experience felt and touched within your heart expanding beyond self, an expression beyond confinement, a sense of natural freedom, clear and aware.

Primordial Grace   The path laid out in your heart and the fabric of being for blending into essence. The sacred intent of divine love arising from the heart of origin. The great perfection woven throughout the fabric of being offering always a way home in and through the natural radiance of the origin itself. The practices of opening to this sacred wholeness, the spiritual path of direct experience, the path of Earth, original heart, and the visionary practice of radiance. The call within you and all around you to follow the path of return to origin.

Radiance   The arising weave of the fabric of being. The spontaneous unceasing dynamic expression blossoming forth from the essence, blooming in myriad ways. The great compassion. The intent of the essence manifesting for all beings to mature spiritually and reflect back to origin. The entire world vision we find ourselves within, rocks, trees, plants, waters, sky, the light in every heart, and the primordial visions of radiance all woven of the same strands of living light, the intent of essence.

Return   Fruition of the primordial path that emanates from and returns to essence, just as a circle is drawn. The completion inherent in the path from the beginning. Seamless oneness. The journey of return to origin is through the acknowledging and the final blending. See *Embrace*.

Visionary Path of Radiance   Dynamic visionary process of the four visions of radiance arising from your heart and the very basis of all experience. The primordial path of direct engagement with the radiance of essence, allowing the compassionate and very beautiful expressions of living light encoded in your heart to guide you home to full resolution, blending seamlessly into essence. The path of joy, primordial joy, the pure generative joy of the source present as the path from the beginning, expressed directly as and through the visions of radiance.

Artists Robert and Rachel Olds spent nine years in spiritual retreat together integrating Earth living and the practices of primordial grace. They came to their retreat after years of spiritual inquiry through their artwork and years of letting go and simplifying their lives to connect more fully with the natural world. Through their books, they share their perspective from the completion of the visionary path of radiance to encourage recognition that this Earth, this vision we call life, is a sacred offering.

They offer teachings of direct experience within the natural world for opening to original heart and embracing the radiant expression we call life. Their books include *Luminous Heart of Inner Radiance, Luminous Heart of the Earth,* and *Water Drawn before Sunrise.*

www.acircleisdrawn.org